# NGŨGĨ WA THIONG'O

Ngũgĩ wa Thiong'o is one of the leading writers
and scholars at work in the world today. His books
include the novels *Petals of Blood*, for which
he was imprisoned by the Kenyan government
in 1977, *A Grain of Wheat* and *Wizard of the
Crow*; the memoirs *Dreams in a Time of War*, *In
the House of the Interpreter*, *Birth of a Dream
Weaver* and *Wrestling with the Devil*; and the
essays *Decolonizing the Mind*, *Something Torn
and New* and *Globaletics*. Recipient of many
honours, among then ten honorary doctorates,
he is currently distinguished professor of English
and Comparative Literature at the University of
California, Irvine.

T0332821

# Praise for *The Perfect Nine*

'A beautiful work that not only refuses distinctions between "high art" and traditional storytelling, but supplies that all-too-rare human necessity: the sense that life has meaning'
*Guardian*

'*The Perfect Nine* uses a deceptively simple language that lays bare deep truths'
*Financial Times*

'A vivid, exhilarating tale with a surprisingly modern philosophy that emphasises the importance of tolerance, feminism and respect for the environment'
*Mail on Sunday*

'As pacy and addictive as it is measured. Thick with allegory and adventure . . . this is a beautifully told epic about the fundamentals of humanity'
*New Statesman*

'In this sinuous retelling by the great Kenyan writer, the founding myth of the Gĩkũyũ people emerges as an epic poem rivalling *The Iliad* in body count and surpassing it in whimsy'
*New Yorker*

'Unfolding in wry and lyrical verse, *The Perfect Nine* tells a Homeric odyssey of the creation of the entire Gĩkũyũ people – a creationist myth, an adventure tale and a family story, wherein the wives do not simply wait at home'
*Literary Hub*

'[*The Perfect Nine*] departs from the sprawl of his past novels
into an engaging if slight lyrical epic. Combining Homeric
verse with oral storytelling tropes – choruses, chants, songs –
he retells the origin myth of the Gĩkũyũ, Kenya's largest
tribe . . . Ngũgĩ wa Thiong'o's fans will appreciate this'
*Publishers Weekly*

'Ngũgĩ wa Thiong'o's first venture into epic poetry is a
triumph of the form, which resounds with the lyrical
heartbeat of the Gĩkũyũ people in Kenya as [he]
chronicles their mythic history'
*World Literature Today*

'[*The Perfect Nine*'s] sophistication comes from the
use of the narrative voice, which positions the reader
as part of a common humanity'
*London Review of Books*

'Ngũgĩ wa Thiong'o masterfully sings us through an origin
story written in verse. This book is a magisterial and poetic
tale about women's place in a society of Gods. It is also
about disability and how expectations shape and determine
characters' spiritual anchoring'
2021 International Booker Prize Judges

NGŨGĨ WA THIONG'O

# The Perfect Nine

The Epic of Gĩkũyũ and Mũmbi

Translated from the Gĩkũyũ
original by the author

VINTAGE

1 3 5 7 9 10 8 6 4 2

Vintage is part of the Penguin Random House group of companies whose addresses can be found at global.penguinrandomhouse.com

First published in Vintage in 2023
First published in Great Britain by Harvill Secker in 2020
First published with the title *Kenda Mũiyũru* in Kenya
by East African Educational Publishers Ltd in 2018

Copyright © Ngũgĩ wa Thiong'o 2020

Ngũgĩ wa Thiong'o has asserted their right to be identified as the author of this Work in accordance with the Copyright, Designs and Patents Act 1988

penguin.co.uk/vintage

A CIP catalogue record for this book is available from the British Library

ISBN 9781784706784

Printed and bound in Great Britain by Clays Ltd, Elcograf S.p.A.

The authorised representative in the EEA is
Penguin Random House Ireland, Morrison Chambers,
32 Nassau Street, Dublin D02 YH68

Penguin Random House is committed to a sustainable future for our business, our readers and our planet. This book is made from Forest Stewardship Council® certified paper.

# Contents

# Notes on
## *The Perfect Nine:*
## *The Story of Gĩkũyũ and Mũmbi*

THE GĨKŨYŨ ARE ONE OF SEVERAL PEOPLES that make up the Kenyan nation. All of the different peoples have their own language and their own myth of origins (in Gĩkũyũ, the "ũ" is pronounced like the "o" in "boat"; the "ĩ" is pronounced like the "a" in "take").

The Gĩkũyũ people trace theirs to Gĩkũyũ (man) and Mũmbi (woman). God put the pair on the snow-capped Mount Kenya, from where they surveyed the lands around. They made their home in a place called Mũkũrũweinĩ. They had nine daughters, but they were actually ten, hence the Perfect Nine.

Legend has it that when the girls came of marrying age, Gĩkũyũ went back to the mountaintop and asked God to provide. On waking up one morning, the family found ten handsome young men outside their home in Mũkũrũweinĩ. The ten clans of the Gĩkũyũ people are named after the ten daughters.

The epic *The Perfect Nine* is an interpretation of that myth starting from a question: where did the Ten Suitors come from? I imagined them as the last left standing after others failed tests of character and resolve.

The daughters, having grown up without brothers, had to depend on themselves. They had to acquire all the skills of survival: defend themselves, work the land, build and make things, including houses, clothes, weapons. Self-reliance was central to their character. Theirs was the union of mind, heart, and hands. They embodied wholesome beauty. The Perfect Nine would seem to be the original feminists.

I use the quest for the beautiful, as an ideal of living, as the motive force behind migrations of African peoples. The epic came to me one night as a revelation of ideals of quest, courage, perseverance, unity, family, and the sense of the divine, in human struggles with nature and nurture.

# Prologue

I will tell the tale of Gīkūyū and Mūmbi
And their daughters, the Perfect Nine,
Matriarchs of the House of Mūmbi,
Founders of their nine clans,
Progenitors of a nation.

I will tell of their travels, and
The countless hardships they met on the way,
Tremor after tremor raging from the belly of the
    earth,
Eruptions breaking the ground around them,
Making the ridges quake, the earth tremble, as

New hills heaved themselves out of the earth, and
Others burned, their flames flaring skyward,
And valleys formed deep and wide behind them.
When Gīkūyū and Mūmbi looked back, and
Saw a river of thick red mud moving toward them,

They climbed other ridges,
Any that seemed free of flames, but

Just as they sought to sit down
For a much needed rest,
They saw a big red rock,

Hurtling down toward them,
Forcing them back on their heels and down to the
	plains.
Other fires flared up in front of them, and again
they were back on their feet, beating a hasty retreat,
Looking for any place that would offer respite.

They faced hazards big enough to shatter the hearts
	of many.
Their bodies trembled, but their hearts remained
	unshaken,
For Gĩkũyũ and Mũmbi had robed themselves with
	hope
And fastened themselves with courage and moved
	on.

And then they came to a mountain
Whose top touched the sky.
How they were able to climb it, they could not
	fathom,
But they found themselves at the top,
Where now they stood, awed by

The summit, as white and massive as the moon,
Its coldness pushing them back as if
Commanding them to stop.
They exchanged fleeting glances, not knowing
Whether to advance or retreat.

Before them spread the chilling whiteness,
Threatening to freeze their hearts;
Behind them the sluggish red rivers of fire,
And the earth convulsing,
And the molten rock rolling down toward them.

They did not let hope die.
They did not ask, "Why us?"
Or indulge in blaming each other.
They held firm, and
Cast their eyes ahead to find the way.

Far beyond, they sighted another mountain
With a moon-white top, like this one,
As if the two mountains were born of one mother.
And they said, "Another Mountain of the Moon."
They saw yet other mountains,

Lying side by side like the folds of a cowhide in the
    sun.

They cried out, "Look, the mountains of the cow-
    hides!"
There were others shaped like turtle beans.
And they named them the Njahī Bean Mountains.
Still others, the Mbirūirū—Blue-Black—Mountains.

The landscape was beautiful.
For a moment they were at a loss for words to
    describe
The undulating plains that spread out before them,
    or
The hills and valleys that hedged them in, or
The rivers that flowed through the green lilies and
    reeds.

Countless animals of different shapes and colors
Bent low over the waters, drinking and lowing and
    grunting and roaring in delight;
Others strutted about the banks or simply basked
    in the sun.
Gīkūyū and Mūmbi turned to each other and mur-
    mured something.
They were captives to their wonder.

They resumed gazing at the peaceful, green land
    below.

Then they stretched forth their arms in grateful
reverence.
"We receive this with all our hearts, O Giver Su-
preme," they said in unison.
"Thank you, Owner of the Ostrich Whiteness, for
this land, which
You have given us, our children, and our children's
children."

They scooped some of the moonwhite in their hands.
They scattered it on the earth around them.
They started facing north and chanted,
"Peace! Glory to thee, Giver Supreme. Peace!"
Then they turned to the south, and they said,

"Peace! Glory to thee, Giver Supreme. Peace!"
Then they turned to the east, the land of the rising
sun.
"Peace! Glory to thee, Giver Supreme. Peace!"
And last, the west, the land of the setting sun.
"Peace! Glory to thee, Giver Supreme. Peace."

And suddenly they felt their souls stir and soar with
joy.
They recalled the other places they had journeyed
through,

Some of them with mountains and woodlands like
    these,
Rivers like these, animals like these,
But their hearts had not been drawn to them.

And now all the beauty they had left behind
Has reappeared tenfold for them to reap.
More gratitude to the Giver Supreme welled up
    inside,
And they broke into hymns of praise:

*Owner of Ostrich whiteness, we praise you*
*For this brightness that shines so,*
*This soil, these rivers, and the numerous hills,*
*And animals of varied shapes and color.*

*These flowers reflect your glory.*
*The plants and the animals and the birds*
*And the creatures that dwell in rivers and lakes—*
*All creation reflects your glory.*

*We listened and heard the voice.*
*It was you telling us that you have trusted us*
*With this beauty to tend it with care and love*
*Because this wonder manifests your glory.*

. . .

The forests and the mountains echoed with
The melodies and the words and the rhythms.
Voices from all things mingled in the air;
Birds hopped on branches with delight;
Monkeys hung from branches excitedly.

Gĩkũyũ and Mũmbi descended the mountain.
They did not stop to look back.
When fatigue finally caught up with them,
They lay on the ground and slept for nine months,
The big deep sleep of the beginning.

Chirping nyagathanga birds woke them.
In the mũkũrwe and mũkũyũ trees,
The birds hopped up and down in their nests, let-
    ting forth their rapturous song,
As if whistling advice to the man and woman that
They too should set up their own nest there, under
    the trees.

They felt as if born again.
Mũmbi picked a leaf of the mũkũyũ, the fig tree:
"Because you have woken up to a new life,
I, with this mũkũyũ leaf, now rename you son of
    mũkũyũ,
Calling you Mũgĩkũyũ. . . ."

They stopped by a wild olive tree, a mūtamaiyū.
Gīkūyū picked some maiyū leaves.
He sniffed at them and felt good.
"You are still the Mūmbi who molded my heart,
    but
In the name of these leaves, I will also call you my
    Mūtamaiyū."

They started playing with the names,
Trying different variations,
Different nicknames,
Till they ended with
"Husband! Wife!" they called out in unison.

They exchanged glances,
Their eyes sending out light,
Dwellers in a dreamland.
Then they turned to the earth:
"Peace! Glory be to thee, Giver Supreme. Peace!

They then turned to the mountain of ostrich white-
    ness and
Chanted gratitude to the Giver Supreme
For bringing them to Mūkūruweinī.
They sang more hymns of gratitude

For their safe deliverance under the Mūkūrūweinī
   shrine.

*Owner of Ostrich Whiteness, we praise you*
*For this brightness around us,*
*This soil, these rivers and numerous hills,*
*And these animals of different kinds.*

Even I, teller of this tale, will first do the same:
Implore the Giver Supreme to bestow peace in my
   heart, so that
I can render this tale of Gīkūyū and Mūmbi and
   their Perfect Nine,
Exactly the way the wind whispered it to my soul,
   when once
I stood on a hill watching swallows flying in the air.

# Supplication for Power to the Tongue

Peace! May all glory be to thee, Giver Supreme.
Peace! May all glory be to thee, Giver Supreme.
In some parts of Africa, they call it Mulungu, but it
  is the same Giver.
The Zulu call him Unkulunkulu, but he is the same
  Giver.
Others call it Nyasai, Jok, Oldumare, Chukwu, or
  Ngai, but each is the same Giver.
The Hebrews call upon Yahweh or Jehovah, and he
  is the same Giver.
Mohammedans call Him Allah, and he is the same
  Giver.

God has many names, and they all point to the
  Giver Supreme.
In ancient Egypt they saw God manifest in the
  trinity of
Osiris,
Isis,
Horus.

. . .

The trinity appears in many states of being:
Father,
Mother,
Child.
The trinity of Birth.

Birth,
Life,
Death.
The trinity of Life.

Morning,
Noon,
Evening.
The trinity of Day.

Yesterday,
Today,
Tomorrow.
The trinity of Time.

Time flows on like an endless river,
Time Yesterday into Time Today,
Time Today into Time Tomorrow.

. . .

Now is Now and it is not Now because Time does
   not stop.
Yesterday is Yesterday and it is not Yesterday be-
   cause Time did not stop.
Tomorrow is Tomorrow and it is not Tomorrow
   because Time will not stop.

Day is the seamless union of Yesterday Today To-
   morrow.
Today arrives from Yesterday carrying Tomorrow
   within itself:
The intertwinement of Time.

The past and the past of the past and
The future of the future are a continuum:
The Circle of Life.

God is Life.
God is One.
Life is One.

One is the beginning of all creation;
One is the One sought by Egyptian sages
And the Greeks and the Hebrews and all seekers of
   the

One that connects the soil and the sea and Earth
And the space-worlds we see above
And the many other space-worlds we cannot see
  with our eyes.

In those space-worlds dwell suns and moons and
  stars,
The ones we see and many others we don't see,
Home to the stars that light the night and show the
  way.

One is the beginning of the many.
The journey of a thousand miles begins with one
  step.
Never look down upon a drop of rain.

God is water.
God is soil.
God is air.
God is sun.

God is the Thing itself:
The thing in the human,
The thing in the thing,
The thing in the place,
The thing in the matter,

The thing in all things—
Because that Thing is in everything everywhere.

Among the Agĩkũyũ, it is called Mulungu,
The Owner of Ostrich Whiteness.
God has many names but they all point to the same
    Giver Supreme.

Let us now sing:

*God is darkness and light.*
*He is the being and the nonbeing.*
*She is the stars and the moon and the sun*
*And all the spaces in between.*
*God is the past of the past*
*And the past before the past.*
*God is the eternal present.*
*God is the tomorrow of tomorrow.*
*He is distance; he is nearness.*
*She is the here and the there and the everywhere.*
*God is Giver Supreme but It cannot be divided,*
*For It is the Giver Supreme.*
*He multiplies himself and gives himself.*
*She gives herself to the soil and the water and wind.*
*It gives itself to plants and animals and birds and*
    *creatures of the sea.*

*She is the beginning of all beginnings*
*He is the end of all ends,*
*But the end is the beginning*
*The earth and below-the-earth are hers because she*
   *is the earth.*
*The heavens and the heavens above the heavens are*
   *his because he is the heavens.*
*God is everywhere every time all the time.*

Glory to God, the Giver Supreme.
Glory to God, the Giver Supreme.

Sharing is the commandment of the Giver Su-
   preme.
Helping one another is the commandment of the
   Giver Supreme.
Supporting one another is the commandment in all
   creation.

No organ of the body is sufficient unto itself.
They work together because they know that,
In helping the others, they help themselves.

Glory to the Giver Supreme.
Glory to the Giver Supreme,
The Giver without and within us all.

3

The
Perfect
Nine

I implore thee for the power to faithfully tell this
     tale of Gĩkũyũ and Mũmbi,
Which is also the tale of their daughters, the Per-
     fect Nine,
How news of their beauty spread to all the earth
     and
Made men take up cudgels and swords to settle
     disputes over
The beautiful ones, whose beauty they had not yet
     set eyes upon.

Those who had eaten more salt in this world tried
     to broker peace:
Lay down your swords, young men. The beautiful
     one will always be born.
Reasoning with the heart is better than rioting
     with the sword.
Win hearts with good deeds, not with golden
     swords.
The Perfect Nine are the matriarchs of the nine
     clans of Gĩkũyũ and Mũmbi.

I will start by calling out their names, one by one:
Wanjirū, Wambūi, Wanjikū, Wangūi, and
    Waithīra aka Wangeci,
Waceera, Nyambura aka Mwīthaga, Wairimū,
    Wangarī aka Waithiegeni—and Wamūyū,
Who completes the nine to make the Perfect Nine.
They are the matriarchs of the nine clans; and
Each clan has traits traceable back to the matriarch.

## Wanjirū, Matriarch of the Anjirū Clan

Of the Perfect Nine, she is the oldest.
Her clan swears by the name Njirū.
It is said she once put a curse on a hyena,
But she had simply put a curse on greed.
Her face exudes empathy and goodness, and
She does not falter when fighting for peace;
She swears by her clan as she calls for conflicts to
    cease.
When visitors descend upon her from anywhere,
She says, "Don't ask hunger questions. First give it
    food."
Her beauty makes men fight to walk beside her.

## *Wambūi, Matriarch of the Mbūi Clan*

Do they say Wambūi sold away a son in a time of
  famine?
No, she sent him to fetch food for people in a time
  of famine.
He returned with a basket full of eatables and, after
  people were satisfied, exclaimed:
"A boy has done as well as a girl, and now we are
  full. Truly
A boy and a girl are equally able to fend for the
  nation."
Wambūi weaves baskets reading the stars.
She once rode a zebra to war and led an army to
  victory,
For when the enemy saw black and white stripes
  shining in the plains,
They put down their swords and fled.
When she passes, men nearly break their necks as
  they strain to look at her.
Her clan swears by her name, Wambūi.

## *Wanjikū, Matriarch of the Agacikū Clan*

Her clan swears by the name Wanjikū.
She loves work, says it never killed anybody.
They claim she grows enough millet to feed a
    nation.
She fights back so fiercely, some people claim she
    provokes the fights.
She cherishes her personal freedom and self-
    reliance, so much that
Those driven by envy call her selfish.
She hates the bewitching words of falsehood.
She knows all about herbs that heal the body.
She also possesses healing powers of peace.
She is so beautiful, none can take their eyes off her.

## *Wangũi, Matriarch of the Thiegeni Clan*

Her clan swears by their name in hers, Ngũi.
It is said she came out her mother's womb singing.
Even in a baby carrier, she would sing lullabies to
　　her mother.
That was why she is called Wangoi and Wangũi.
It is said that once she sang in the courtyard, and
Birds crowded the nearest trees and bushes to hear
　　her.
Her voice once made fighters put down their
　　swords to first hear;
By the time the song was over, they had forgotten
　　all about the fight.
Her beauty made many a neck strain with pain as
　　men turned to look at her.
That is why some people also called her Wangũi the
　　neck-breaker.

## *Waithīra, Matriarch of the Thīra Clan*

She is also called Wangeci.
Her clan swears by the name Ngeci.
She once cleared so much forest, her machete broke.
She indulges in humor only after she has completed
    her tasks.
Waithīra does not engage in rumors and hearsay;
She likes to know all the facts before settling on an
    option.
She likes resolving, not just listening to problems.
She does not favor one side or the other;
She listens to both carefully before she decides.
She is a beauty. Men fake being hot with fever,
So that she can touch them to feel their tempera-
    ture.

## Njeri, Matriarch of the Cera Clan

They say a Mūceera clansperson shuns company.
Yes, the company of those without character.
And that she brings down bananas with the power
    of a glance?
Yes, but they fall down from the weight of ripeness,
From the care she has given them.
Njeri reasons in search of justice.
Those who seek the right way sing to her:
"Arm me with reason so that I can find the middle
    way.
Njeri, please visit black people with the ointment
    of blessings."
A glance at her beauty makes men bent over work
    feel rested.
Her clan swears by her name.

## Mwĩthaga, Matriarch of the Ethaga Clan

They gave her the name for the colors she wears,
But her clan swears by her other name, Nyambura,
A name given her for her rainmaking powers.
They say a Mwĩthaga gets rich at night, yes, because,
Every night, she reviews events of the day and
    makes plans for tomorrow.
She uses her powers to brings down hawks that
    threaten her chickens.
She uses her powers to drive away foxes and hyenas
    that pose threats to her goats.
For this, some claim that her eyes have the power to
    bewitch.
She, too, seeks reason in the service of justice.
She is so beautiful that birds whistle admiration as
    she passes.

## Wairimũ, Matriarch of the Thigia Clan

Her clan swears by her name Wairimũ.
She tends plants and potato vines to abundance.
She makes pots, like her mother, but she adds deco-
    rations;
She invents things, like her father, but she adds
    patterns to them.
She sculpts things or animals so vividly,
Her detractors say she traps the souls of things and
    people.
She drinks what she milks, eats what she has grown,
    wears what she has made.
She hates foolishness! And when it comes to throw-
    ing spears, she's among the best.
Her beauty makes men change direction to follow
    her, which
Makes some claim it's because of the likenesses she
    draws and sculpts.

## Wangarī, Matriarch of the Ngarī Clan

Her clan swears by the name Wangarī.

She has the courage of a leopard; her eyes are similarly bright.

She has the quickness of a leopard in protecting the powerless from the powerful.

She is wily; she once called off work so that people would rest and feast;

When they resumed, they did the work with care, diligence, and love.

She once threw a firebrand at a leopard; it ran away and left the herd alone.

She says that disagreements that sharpen the mind are the whetstones of life,

But disagreements that sharpen the sword are whetstones of death.

Her beauty once made a young man cover his hand with cloth,

So that the warmth from her handshake would not escape or evaporate.

## Warigia, Matriarch of Mūyū Clan

Her other name, Wamūyū, has the same roots as
    Gīkūyū,
But she is also known as Wanjūgū for playing
    among beans and peas.
Warigia, the Last One, is also her name, for she was
    the last born.
She is often missing when the nine are mentioned,
Because, some so claim, she gave birth, unmarried,
    at her parents' home.
Surprised by her unerring marksmanship, some say
    she has occult powers.
Otherwise, how can a child born with crippled legs
Be so good with arrows?
It is said that her teeth were so white they lit a path
    in the darkness.
When she laughs, even animals follow suit.
Her clan swears by the name Mūyū.
With her, the nine daughters become ten, the Per-
    fect Nine.

4
—

# The Wind and the Ostrich

The nine were born under the shadow of Mount
    Kenya.
Nine ostriches flew from their sacred base at the top
    of the mountain.
They rode horselike on the waves of the wind,
In the eight directions of the wind and one toward
    the center,
With nine trumpets, announcing the birth of the
    beauty that

Later spread into all things we call beautiful.
The fame of their beauty spread to Ethiopia and
    Egypt and other regions.
Young men lost sleep in dreams of the beautiful
    ones, and
Each would secretly leave in pursuit of the image in
    his dreams,
Each following whatever river he first came across.

Some followed the White Nile, with origins in
    Nyanza;

Others followed the Blue Nile, with origins in
  Tana.
Others followed Niger, rumored to flow under-
  ground from the Nile.
To others, the Senegal, the Congo, Bangui, and
  Kasai were their rivers of promise.
Another group trusted their dreams to Orange and
  Limpopo and Zambesi.


When the river led to a cul-de-sac, they trekked
  through forest and mountains.
The ladies of Egypt and those lands followed their
  young men,
Not believing that mountains could produce beau-
  ty to rival that born of water.
Beauty born of a mountain—how can it beat the
  beauty born of water?


Water.
Earth.
Air.
Sun.
Which of them is the fountain of life?


Sun brings heat and light.
It divides day and night.

It makes plants and trees breathe in and out.
The fumes rise to the heavens and become dark
  clouds.

The clouds become pregnant.
They let down rain.
The earth drinks the water.
Plants grow roots.
They bear leaves and flowers.
They bask in the sun.
And so on, one thing to the other,
The circle of life.

Water.
Earth.
Air.
Sun.

Among water, earth, air, and sun, there is no supe-
  rior.
Together, they make the primal seed of life.
Life is one:
Humans, animals, birds, worms, creatures of the
  sea—
Every being takes its share from the common ocean
  of life.

There were many who lost their way, and
Wherever their journey came to an end, they would
plant a spear.
And when a daughter of the waters caught up with
them,
They felt as if their dream had come true.
They built a home to give birth to new dreams.

It was the search for the beautiful, the sacred, and the
secure
That gave Africa different peoples, clans, and settle-
ments.
Ninety-nine finally reached Mount Kenya,
As if they had prior agreement on where to finally
meet, or
As if an unknown power had driven them to
Mūkūrūweinī.

An arrow whistled in the air and landed at the feet of
those in front.
They stopped, each holding firm his weapons,
Ready to defend themselves against an invisible enemy,
But from all sides, the arrows continued to rain down,
Barely missing their legs and toes.

. . .

They stared front, back, and sides, but they could
    not see the enemy.
And then they heard a voice command them to lay
    down their spears,
And all the other weapons they held, and place
    them under a tree.
Obediently, they put down all their spears and
    swords and clubs.
Then they saw an elderly man and woman standing
    before them:

He wore a cloak colobus monkey hide;
He held a staff in his hands, and from his earlobes
    hung large earrings.
The woman wore copper rings around her neck and
    hands, and
A long brown leather skirt and dangling colorful
    earrings.
In her hand she held a sword and a long-necked
    gourd.

Their eyes seemed fixed to beyond the strangers,
But their stance looked peaceful.
Is it possible that it was these elderly folk
Who rained the arrows from all sides and from
    above?

"Have you come in peace or war?" the old man
    asked.

Before the men could answer, a young woman
    appeared before them.
She wore leather gowns and bead earrings and
Necklaces and copper rings around the neck.
She held a bow and arrow; on her back hung a
    quiver of arrows.
She seemed ready to launch an arrow at them, but
    her face was enigmatic.

Was the face that of one about to laugh or about to
    wage war?
Before they could fathom the mystery, they saw
    more beauties appear.
Some stood in front, others to the sides, but all
    equally armed to the teeth.
After the men had fed their eyes to the full with the
    sight of the beautiful braves,
They knew that they had indeed arrived at their
    destiny.

Their fears vanished;
Their fatigue evaporated;
Hunger too,

Thirst as well.
What they really saw was their dreams come true.

They embarked on new dreams,
Only now they did not know if these were real or
    not,
Because before the men made themselves known
Or engaged in any preliminaries,
They lay under the nearest trees and slept.

5

# Feast
# Song
# and
# Dance

"When sleep calls, you don't say to it, 'Let's first
    talk,'" Gīkūyū said.
Looking back to his own travels with Mūmbi,
He saw his own youth in these young men.
"It is hunger that's impatient with talk," Njeri said
    to her father.
"Yes, you soothe it with food, not words," Mūmbi
    and the others agreed.

The nine daughters went into the forest to hunt,
To get enough meat to prepare for the sleeping
    ninety-nine.
Some other days they went to the fields to gather
    foods to
Cook for the ninety-nine guests,
Who were still snoring, dead asleep.

After nine days, the men woke up, one after
    another.
Gīkūyū showed them where to gather. He talked to
    them:

"The newcomer is the one who brings news,
But we all agreed that one cannot get many words
    from the sleeping.
Hunger is impatient with small talk, so off to the
    river you go.
When you come back, we shall take care of your
    thirst and hunger.

The nine girls led the men down the valley to the
    river, with song:
*Flow, river, flow, but don't flow with me. I want you
    to wash me, not wash me away.*
They took off their outer garments, leaving their
    underwear
And bead necklaces that fell beautifully over their
    chests.
Waithīra was the first to jump into the river, near
    the waterfall.

Singly or with others, the rest followed, and
When the men, all ninety-nine, saw this,
They also took off their garments and jumped into
    the waters.
After they were cleansed, they went back to the
    homestead,
Where they found mountains of food:

. . .

Meat, sweet potatoes, yams, arrowroots, millet, sor-
  ghum, porridge, and herbal wine.
Mwĩthaga called upon the rain to give them time to
  entertain the guests before it fell.
The rain and the wind heard her pleas and let the sun
  rule undisturbed.
The guests and the hosts listened to the music float-
  ing from the bushes,
An orchestra of crickets, birds, and frogs, with howls
  from the big animals.

Even as they ate and drank, the youths were eyeing
  one another.
Wangũi sang a song of welcome.
Birds flew down from the trees and landed in the yard,
Where they mixed with humans without fear.
Even the animals of the forest pricked up their ears
  and listened.

And now Gĩkũyũ stood up again: "What did I say?
It is the newcomer who brings news of the outside.
You have eaten and whatever remains awaits you.
So, what news do you bring to this homestead?
The people from whom you have come, how do they
  dance?"

The men took up the challenge,
Each man and the dance of his region of origin,
Or a dance and song he had picked up on the way.
Others took to makeshift drums
And flutes or simply clapped and whistled.

Each man came up with amazing steps.
Some jumped in the air and twisted their bodies
As if they had no bones to worry about,
Each one trying to outdo the others.
And the women clapped and ululated in joy.

In the evening, the women made a bonfire.
The light from the flames blended with that of the
    moon and the stars.
This was the time for stories about their different
    adventures.
The women had their mouths open in wonder and
    amazement.
Days came and went: feasting in daytime, storytell-
    ing in the evening.

But one evening, instead of a story, Gĩkũyũ spoke
    to the gathering thus:

"Now that you have rested, feasted, and danced,
  you can tell us:
What really brought you from all the corners of the
  wind to these parts?
Or did the hurricane carry you in the air like leaves,
And when the wind lost power, let you fall down
  into this yard?"

One by one they spoke, but the song was really the
  same:
It was the fame of the beauty of these nine that
  brought them there.
Word of their beauty had reached them wherever
  they lived.
At night, alone, each saw a silhouette of a beauty in
  dreams,
And even in daytime, the silhouette would not go
  away.

If one tried to catch the image, she slipped away in
  mockery,
Tantalizing him with the softness of black beauty,
And with eyes that shone bright like stars at night.
Without telling anyone, they undertook the jour-
  ney of quest.

· · ·

Some met on the road, all bent on the same mission,

Toward the destiny intimated in their dreams.
And when, after so many trials, they finally arrived,
They found that the beauty in their dreams had
    deceived them,
Because now they saw with their own eyes that
The beauty in reality was more than any they had
    seen in their dreams.

"So you came here to feed your eyes on beauty,"
    Mũmbi asked,
"So that when you return home you'll have tales to
    tell?"
"No, no, we did not come here to collect tales to tell
    later."
They each had the one desire to capture the heart of
    one of the nine
And take her home to create new clans.

Suddenly they heard laughter in the dark.
None had ever heard a laughter that carried so
    much joy.
And now they saw some teeth and two eyes shining
    in the dark,

But when the light of the fire lit up the owner of the
    laughter,
They were taken aback by the sight of a grown
    woman creeping.

"Warigia is my last born," Mũmbi explained.
    "She makes up the Perfect Nine.
Her eyes can see a long way, and her ears hear
    sounds from afar.
Her legs are the only organs that remained those of
    a child.
The rest of the body is a grown woman, and she
    does things her own way.
She said she would take her time to see and hear
    you."

"Now you have seen them all," Gĩkũyũ said.
The nine have become the Perfect Nine.
You are ninety-nine.
Where shall I get other tens to meet your needs?
Or do you want each of the nine to end with nine
    of you?

# 6

## Gĩkũyũ
## and
## Mũmbi

One man stood up, body trembling with rage.
He could hardly manage to get a word out.
"Every one of us suitors owns a sword and a club.
Let's fight among ourselves. The blows will help sort
out the worthy.
The nine suitors who remain standing will have the
nine."

And with the last word, he took out his sword,
And he strutted about, raging like a fighting bull,
Muttering threats, fueled by the desire to fight and
conquer.
The others pulled out their swords and shouted chal-
lenges,
Ninety-nine swords shining bright in the dark.

A while ago they were bathing together and sharing
meals;
Now they looked more like enraged animals, fangs out,
Each claiming the region he came from as more spe-
cial than the others,

That his people were the elect of God,
That their God was the true God.

"What is this stupidity in full display?" asked
   Wairimū.
"You come here, from wherever you did, to bring us
   this foolishness?
War among yourselves? Are you not mature men?
Why war among the same people?
Did you come here for Love or War?"

Her sisters ululated in support of her wise words.
Wangūi started a song.
The others joined in.
The rage in the suitors' hearts subsided;
They put their swords back in their scabbards.

*Mūmbi said:*
"My name is Mūmbi, like
The creator of pots,
The creator of forms,
The creator of character,
The creator of the created."

*Gīkūyū said:*
"Mūmbi who made me her captive,

Mũmbi who landed in my heart,
Mũmbi who wins hearts with reason,
Mũmbi who revels in truth and peace.
Let Mũmbi share more of her wisdom."

*Mũmbi said:*
"I carried the Perfect Nine in my womb,
Each for nine months,
All in all, ninety months.
In my house blood will not be spilled over any of
    the nine,
Unless that of a goat for food or blessings."

*Gĩkũyũ said:*
"We all have descended from the same humans.
We inherited their humanity,
Which now is ours to cherish, nourish, and pass on,
But there are always those intent on scuttling it.
They may dwell among us or come from the out-
    side.

"To build calls for hard work,
From the one who looks to tomorrow.
To destroy is easy work,
For one who wants to return to yesterday,
Like a grown person wishing to remain a child.

"War destroys lives.
Peace restores lives.
The warrior and the warrior bring home trophies of
    tears.
The peacemaker and peacemaker bring home tro-
    phies of laughter.
My only one and I came from far places in search of
    peace.

"We started as a large group,
Some in flight from senseless wars,
Others from other unsavory challenges, and
Others driven by desire to know what lay beyond.
The human is driven by the quest for love or knowl-
    edge.

"We journeyed toward the Mountains of the Moon,
Their brightness calling us the way the nine lured
    you here,
Some lost their way or stopped to build new villages.
In the end, we two remained; we stayed together,
Young blood, our hearts beating with hope.

"Maybe one day we and the others will unite,
    because

All people born of humans,
Who know themselves to be human offspring—
They are our siblings, members of the human clan,
Yes, proud sons and daughters of the human.

"Come, let us embrace in friendship.
Come, let us drink together in friendship.
Come, let us share a meal together.
Come one, come all. Let us help one another.
Every human is human because of other humans.

"That's why we have welcomed your visit, because
It enriches the human in us, which makes the human
    human.
In welcoming you, we embraced the human within us,
But we were also ready to protect our humanity,
Ensure it is not torn apart by the enemies of the
    human.

"The human, like the divine, has many names, but its
    real name is Human.
The human is everywhere in all things earthly,
    because
The thing in the human is the thing in all things.
The thing in the human is the thing in place, the
    thing in time: the thing in itself.

The Thing in all things is what causes the thing in
    the human be a human thing.

"Mũmbi and I have come a long way from afar,
Climbed impassable hills and mountains,
Walked down steep valleys.
We have walked through valleys of fire;
We have swum across rivers of fire."

*Mũmbi asked:*
"Have you ever seen hills heave themselves out of
    the belly of the earth?
Have you ever had to run barely a step ahead of red
    rocks of fire?
Have you ever seen a river suddenly gush out of a
    mountainside—
Molten red porridge flowing down slowly but
    relentlessly?
Have you ever heard of the dragon of the waters?"

*Gĩkũyũ said:*
"We saw it, once, its mouth raised above the
    water,
The body hidden in the waters, which spread to
    beyond the ken's eye.

It weaved waves that spread from here to the hori-
zon, but
Near the land, the waves splashed foams white as
anything
And then vomited white anger on the shore."

*Mūmbi said:*
"Sometimes it sent water up the skies into an arch
of a rainbow.
That was also why we ran to the safety of the moun-
tains,
And even there, you have heard of the wonders that
befell us:
Fiery rocks vomited out of the side belly of the
mountains,
And rivers the color of blood gushing down the
valleys."

*Gīkūyū said:*
"We looked for food together.
We hunted animals together.
Sometimes the animals would chase us;
Other times we would chase them.
Young men, how can I tell this tale?"

*Mũmbi said:*
"Once we collapsed with fatigue.
Then we saw a creature bigger than an elephant.
It had seven horns, seven legs, and seven eyes and
Seven ears, seven noses, and seven heads.
It came toward us, its seven mouths wide open,

"And just as we thought this our journey's end,
A big shadow came and covered us."
"It was a bird the bigness of which I had never
    seen," said Gĩkũyũ.
"It encircled our two bodies with claws, picked us
    up," Mũmbi said,
"And flew with us, and eventually dropped us onto
    earth, and went away."

"We have seen all that and more," Gĩkũyũ said.
"And Mũmbi endured it all
And kept in step with me in everything,
Throwing stones, wielding cudgels, spears, or
    arrows—
Whatever I did, she did, my partner in everything.

"I don't know how we ever got to the mountaintop
    or
The power that brought us here without a scar.

And like you, on arrival, we immediately fell asleep.
We slept for nine months,
Covered by a warm blanket of peace.

"Is there anything more blessed than peace?
We woke up and found ourselves under that tree,"
    he said,
And stopped to point in the direction of
    Mūkūrūwe,
"And as we woke up, Mūmbi picks a fight with me,
Challenging me to see who is stronger.

"We wrestled all day,
Weighing each other."
*(He stopped and once again pointed at the tree.)*
"There under that tree we overcame each other,
A thousand birds watching our play.

You, too, the same.
You are ninety-nine men and the Perfect Nine.
My daughters will do the choosing.
But there is only one thing they cannot choose.
My daughters will not go away and leave us here
    alone."

*Mũmbi said:*

"Yes, I shall want to play with my grandchildren and
   even my great-grands.

When people age, they need looking after, the way they
   looked after the children,

The ones once nurtured now nurturing the ones who
   once nurtured them.

If you take our nine away, do you expect us to be mak-
   ing journeys to visit them?

Or you the same, journeying from afar to come to see us?"


*Warigia said:*

"Don't let worry disturb you.

Let my sisters go away if they so wish.

I am your last born.

I am not going anywhere.

I pledge to stay here with you to take care of you in
   your old age."


*Mũmbi said:*

"It's true you are our last born,

But you are all bound by the same rules.

There is no favorite, we love you equally,

And no matter how much your legs deny you motion,

You are still one of the Perfect Nine."

*Gĩkũyũ said (directing his voice at the guests):*
"My soul is large; it welcomes the world.
He who finally links hands with one of these . . . we
  become kin.
*People* make the world, not just the soil. What did
  we say?
A human is human because of the other humans.
All people are people because of other people.

"That is the meaning of greetings.
Your hand and my hand shake in a union of friend-
  ship.
Small and big, man and woman, husband and wife,
We build a new community, a new tomorrow.
He who does not accept that ruling, let him leave in
  peace."

*One man stood up and said:*
"I came from my place to carry mine back home.
I came to marry to take away, not to be taken in."
Another three agreed; four others joined them.
The eight took their weapons and left.

*Gĩkũyũ said:*
"Now ninety-one suitors remain,
Ninety-one in pursuit of the nine.

My daughters will not choose blindly.
Time and deeds alone make people know one
   another.
Let us retire for the night. We meet tomorrow for
   some tests."


The next morning, he took them to see the houses,
As if the guests had not seen them properly.
They were two big huts and a granary full of har-
   vests.
There was a kraal in two sections, one for cows
And the other for goats and sheep.


"We built these with our hands," Gĩkũyũ told
   them,
"And when the nine came of age, they put up theirs.
They live in their own house, except Warigia, who
   still lives with mother.
All of you will stop sleeping in the open like ani-
   mals, but
You will have to raise your own dwellings."


"There, over there, you will build your own," Mũm-
   bi said.
"As soon as the sun appears in the morning, you
   begin.

By the time the sun goes to sleep, you will have put
    up ten huts.
Nine men into each hut
And each of the huts will be named after one of the
    Perfect Nine."

From inside the mother's house, Warigia shouted.
She did not want any of the huts named after her.
Her own heart was her house.
He whom she allowed to enter it would be the
    one,
And she had already chosen him.

Wambūi showed them where they would cut down
    wood for buildings.
She told them that reverence for all life was one of
    the rules of Gīkūyū and Mūmbi.
To harm plants and animals without good cause
    was to harm life.
Never kill an animal unless in defense of self or to
    satisfy hunger.
And if one uproots a tree, one must plant another
    to replace it.

They divided into groups for the different tasks
    according to their abilities,

Without saying this is women's work or that is
    men's work.
Each group cut down and carried the posts, or reeds
    and grass for thatching.
By sunset nine huts were up, walls, thatched roofs
    and all,
Each hut bearing the name of one of the nine
    except Warigia.

Another day Gīkūyū took them to a shrine,
Located in a different part of the forest.
He pointed to a fireplace of three stones
With red clay and a bellows beside the stones.
"Making things is a matter of hands and eyes," he
    said.
"All my daughters are makers of things."

Mũmbi then took them to another shrine, a site for
    pottery.
"Sculpting with clay is another kind of smithery,"
    she told them.
"We make pots and other clay utensils for various
    uses.
We also make wooden spoons for mashing food in
    the pot

And wooden calabashes and other containers for
   porridge and water."

Yet another day, Gĩkũyũ talked to them again.
"What did I tell you? These nine will make their
   choices.
There are a few hurdles you have to jump so you get
   to know one another.
One can never complain about that which one has
   freely chosen.
The girls will each select ten, from whom the one
   most worthy of her final choice
will emerge. . . ."

# 7

# Trials, Falls, and Triumphs

All this time none of the nine had seemed to favor
    any of the suitors.
But when told to each select any ten suitors for her
    group,
Each found herself pointing to one man as first
    choice.
Dispute erupted among them,
Each claiming that *her* heart had selected him first.

The dispute took a bitter turn; insults followed:
Wanjirū, the evil-eyed one.
Njeri, the evil-tongued one.
Wambūi, maker of evil charms.
Wanjikū, the quarrelsome.

Wairimū, married to foolishness.
Wangarī, the mean-spirited.
Nyambura, the foul-mouthed.
Waithīra, the lazy.
Wangūi, who never grows up.

Warigia did not get caught up in their quarrels.
Her eyes shone brightly on one person, whom she
did not identify.
Gĩkũyũ and Mũmbi were without words.
They had never heard their daughters insult each
other so.
Mũmbi took the nine aside in her hut for admoni-
tion.

"When, where, and how did you learn these insults,
Straying from the paths of right, respect, peace, and
love?
Who said that honest disagreements sharpen the
mind and feed the soul,
But those that sharpen the sword in wrath dull the
mind and kill the soul?"
"Wangarĩ!" they all said.

"Who condemned the hyena in human hearts?"
"Wanjirũ!" they called out together.
"Who said that reason must be rooted in good
words?"
"Wambũi!" they said in unison.
"Who said that her arts are for healing, not killing?"
"Wanjikũ!" they said in unison.

. . .

"Who said that everyone should be given respect?"
"Waithīra!" they said in unison.
"Who rejected foolishness?"
"Wairimū!" they said in unison.
"Who said, 'Let us be the rain that puts out fire?'"
"Mwīthaga!" they said.
"Who has a voice that stops wars?"
  "Wangūi!" they said.
"And who says that we should always take the middle way?"
"Njeri!" they said.

"Yes, because the middle rejects extremes.
Reason sees both sides of the path.
Your father and I have come a long way together.
We have argued with each other and gotten to
  know who we are.
We have tested each other with words that build,
  not those that ruin.

"A good heart is led by a somber head.
Heart, head, and hand work together to the same
  end.
We need another person to tell us what is on our
  back.

We shall go about this matter in a different way.
Let reason be the victor.

"Even though you're not sleeping in them,
The huts they built are named after each of you.
Because you have fought among yourselves,
The *men* will stand by the veranda of the house of
    *their* choice.
In the end, you will choose one from among those
    under your roof.
When the heart finds its target, the head will de-
    cide. Never fight over a man."

Matters went as Mũmbi had said. The men went to
    their roof of choice.
One man moved from roof to roof as if dissatisfied
    with the choices before him.
He ended by choosing one at random.
Now every roof had ten men, at least—
Because Warigia had refused to have a hut in her
    name.

"Since you came to us, you have eaten and drunk
    your fill," Gĩkũyũ said.
"Day has been a time of dancing; night, a time of
    storytelling.

You have been lying on the grass under the bushes
   to sleep,
But now you have roofs under which to shelter,
And they are roofs you have freely chosen.


"This forest around is our source of whatever we eat
   and drink.
The rivers give us water. Clothes we make from
   barks of trees and hides of animals.
All citizens of nature—plants, animals, and birds—
   are our friends.
We talk to them, for every creature and object
   speaks a language.
We now want to test how many languages of nature
   you can speak."


When night came, the girls hid among the trees in
   the dark.
The men were to find them without the aid of any
   light.
Not even one suitor was able to find any of the
   women in the dark.
Each man returned alone, saying it was too dark to
   detect anything,
But by the time they came back, the women were
   close behind them.

Now it was the turn of the men, each group of ten
    at a time.
Wanjirũ's group were the first to hide in the dark.
Wanjirũ found them. They were puzzled: how
    could she see in the dark?
It was the turn of the other groups, one at a time.
The girls were able to find them.

*Gĩkũyũ said:*
"Mũmbi and I discovered the secret long ago:
Trees, fire, wind, human and animal alike—
Everything owns a sound, loud or soft.
Even animal and human steps make sound.
When sound hits a thing, it comes back, an echo."

*Mũmbi said:*
"Yes, everything sends back a sound, however soft.
If you listen to the echo with care, you can tell the
    object that sent it out.
The ear is the eye of the soul: it sorts out the sound
    and the echo
And tells what made the sound, where it is coming
    from.
That is why we tell our daughters to keep their ears
    alert."

The next day's test was a competition in making clothes from
The skins of the animals already slaughtered for food.
They also competed in climbing up trees and swinging from tree to tree,
Making fire by drilling into hard stones or sticks, and
Throwing spears, clubs, stones, and other missiles.

The last day was a test of skills with arrows, Gĩkũyũ told them.
Armed with bows and a quiver of arrows, they followed him.
He took them to a place where stood a tall tree with wide trunk.
In the middle of the trunk near the base of the first branch was the tree's eye,
A round scar without bark.

"I want each group to show my daughters how good they are with arrows—
Each man alone and his marksmanship," Gĩkũyũ said.
"Let us first show you by example what I mean," he added.

Mũmbi and Gĩkũyũ walked back a number of
    steps.
Mũmbi took out an arrow from the quiver and set
    it to the bow.

She then closed one eye, pulled the arrow, and then
    let it go.
The arrow whistled in the air all the way into the
    tree's eye.
Gĩkũyũ did the same. It turned into a competition
    between the two;
Their eyes shone bright as if they'd gone back in
    time to their youth.
The young men started whistling and clapping
    hands in admiration.

"When age arrives, it calls for renewal," Mũmbi
    said.
"It is your turn, young men and women, to show
    your skills."
"But you will not shoot from where we did, for we
    are old," Gĩkũyũ said.
He walked back a few more steps, quite a distance.
"Now, Wanjirũ, it is your turn, you and your
    group."

Wanjirū's group begun to set their bows and arrows.

All the men in her group were able to strike the eye.

Now they turned their eyes to Wanjirū.

She did the same, looked, pulled, and shot into the eye.

The other groups followed, with similar success.

After the equal success of all the groups,

Gīkūyū then walked back several steps and asked them to shoot from there.

This went on for some time with all the groups equal in their success,

And each time, Gīkūyū would increase the distance.

In the end, the distance was such that one could hardly see the eye.

In Wanjirū's group, only one man was able to get the eye,

And as before, Wanjirū was the last to try.

Her arrow whistled in the air and went straight into the eye.

The other groups followed with only one or two men succeeding.

As for the girls, not even one missed the eye.

Gĩkũyũ walked back a few more steps.

All the groups, including the women, failed to reach the eye.

But just as they were about to give up shooting and try something else,

They heard a voice from behind them announce, "My turn."

Suddenly, they heard an arrow whistle all the way into the eye.


Warigia shot one after another, and all her arrows found the eye.

The men looked at each other, wondering how she could do this on crippled legs.

Her own sisters were equally puzzled. When did she learn how to shoot?

The man who'd had difficulties in choosing a hut pulled out the arrows for her.

Laughing out loud, Warigia slung the quiver on her back and crawled home.

8

# Mission to the Mountain of the Moon

It was a cloudless morning; Gĩkũyũ and Mũmbi
    stood together.
Before them were the nine groups, each led by one
    of the daughters,
Even Warigia, who had refused to be in a group,
    was present, seated on her legs.
Gĩkũyũ pointed to the far horizon.
"Do you see that which shines like a white ostrich?
Or like the moon at night or white flowers in a field
    of greens?"

"The ostrich whiteness rests on top of the moun-
    tain," Mũmbi said.
"There, up there, is the place where we received
    blessings, after which
We felt stronger and braver, our hearts welling up
    with hope.
From the mountaintop, our eyes fell on this sprawl-
    ing beauty below,
A land never without food or water or green bush."

"It was a revelation of the divine," Gĩkũyũ said,
"A power more than power was whispering assur-
ance in my ear,
That this land is ours and our children's, for genera-
tions to come,
Belonging to us and all the other peoples who will
neighbor us
Or those with whom we make a pact of eternal
friendship.

"Didn't you, our guests, appear before us from all
corners of the earth? Listen.
Any of you who ends up the choice of one of these,
we become kith and kin.
That is why I pour libations every morning, facing
the Mountain of the Moon.
It is the seat of the Giver Supreme, owner of the
ostrich whiteness you now see.
It was the power of the Giver that finally led us to
Mũkũrũwe wa Nyagathanga.

"And because you are now well stretched and fully
rested,
I will send you on a pilgrimage to the holy moun-
tain,
You and the nine, to walk the walk we once walked,

Follow the paths we once followed,
Drink from the calabash of life from which Mūmbi
    and I drank.

"At the top, you'll scoop some of the moon into a
    gourd.
Look about and you will see a round lake.
You will get some water into the gourd to mix with
    the moon.
I want each group to bring back their own mix of
    water and the moon,
For the libations to bless your new journey into
    your future."

"Yes," added Mūmbi, "the journey leads you to our
    beginnings,
So that as you add to the journey, you'll understand
    what you're adding to.
The journey of life is not a shortcut to knowledge; it
    is a long learning process.
One cannot hurry it, and one does not travel on it
    alone.
In every bag I have put two hardy stones for making
    fire and sounds."

"I will give you one more mission," added Gīkūyū.

"Do you see my youngest daughter?" he asked,
    pointing at Warigia.
"When we realized her legs did not have the power
    of the other organs,
We went to the holy shrine around the fig tree to
    sacrifice and ask for a cure.
I was told the cure lies with Mwengeca the king of
    human-eating ogres,

"That he alone possesses some hair that's a cure-all,
    but
He cannot be seen with human eyes unless he
    reveals himself,
And he is always guarded by hundreds of other
    man-eating ogres.
The hair grows in the very middle of his tongue.
I have looked for him everywhere but have encoun-
    tered only his shadow.
I want you to wrestle him to the ground, capture
    his tongue, and pull out the hair.
The hair that cures all will restore full power to
    Warigia's legs."

9

# The
# Journey

How shall I best tell the story of our journey, except
   by confirming
That we did indeed set out from Mūkūrūweinī
Fully armed with staffs and arrows and spears,
And more, with courage and hope and determina-
   tion?—
We, the nine, with our gourds hanging from our
   sides,
Heading toward the mountain of hope and expec-
   tation.
Some days we could see the moon on the moun-
   taintop.
On others, it was completely covered by clouds.
So thick were some of the forests that
Day and night were equally dark,
Made more so by the flickering lights of the fireflies,
The wandering spirits of the forest.

We began our journey with songs and laughter,
Some of the men claiming that this was not much
   of a journey

Compared to those they had already completed
In pursuit of the beautiful nine,
Their spirits buoyed by the images in the dreams
    they had dreamed,
And their belief that they would one day realize
    their dreams.
If they could be so sustained by mere images in
    dreams,
What about now, when they could actually see the
    moon on the mountain?
Or knowing that you had been to the mountaintop
    and survived?


We came to a river covered with bamboo, reeds,
    and grass.
Our laughing dwindled; our hearts sank and grew
    cold,
After we saw the water swallow the three men in
    front.
We saw just their legs in the air as if diving
And then blood on the surface of the water.
Then we saw many crocodiles on the riverbanks,
And it dawned on us that crocodiles had swallowed
    the three.
We the women wept unceasingly;

Among those swallowed was the man we had once
    fought over.

Even the men were overwhelmed with sorrow,
Some holding back their tears with difficulty,
Others moaning, silent tears down their cheeks,
Yet others shaking uncontrollably.
Some of them said the deaths were a sign from
    above
Warning us not to cross the river, that
If we crossed, we would end up as food for hungry
    crocodiles.
Thirty-some gave up and turned back.
Yes, the journey had many trials and tribulations,
Some small but irritating, like those from
Thorns piercing our bodies,
Stinging nettles burning our bodies,
Legs swelling, coughs, and mucus flowing out of
    our noses.
One time we came across a grass-covered flat plain,
But when we stepped on it, the earth beneath our
    feet wobbled,
So we first dipped sticks into it to see
If the ground was firm enough to walk on.

Wangarī warned us not to walk across it,
But we ignored her because
Some of the men assured us that it was marshland
And, despite the wobble, the ground would hold us.
We had hardly gone halfway when seven others
    sank
As if they had been sucked under by a creature
    below.
We couldn't decide whether to go on or back the
    way we came,
The front and the back being the same distance.

We linked hands and walked in line,
So that if any fell into another hole,
We could pull him out with our combined power.
We were able to cross without another danger,
But once on the other side, sadness struck us
At the memory of the seven we had lost,
Swallowed into the belly of the earth.
The hardest part was the doubts that pierced our
    hearts.
Why were we really doing this? For what? To get
    what?

Some tried to convince us we were heading toward
    our end.

They said they would look for a way back home
And immediately acted on the decision.
They left our hearts with more doubts:
Shall we press on or give up and look for a way
    back?
But the mountain was beckoning us, and
When we recalled all the hardships you once faced
Yet were able to tighten the belt of hope and cour-
    age,
We felt inspired to go for victory.

We walked in daytime. At night we lay down wher-
    ever sleep seized us.
A few days without dangerous encounters, and
    laughter trickled back.
But no sooner did we feel safe than snakes bit two
    men at the heels.
Wanjikū chewed some roots and put the mixture
    on the wounds.
The power of the herbs weakened the snakes' poi-
    son.
Another group said that life was more important
    than love and beauty,
And that beautiful ones were everywhere, even in
    their home regions.
They wouldn't wait to be bitten by other snakes.

They split from us and looked for a way back to
    their homes.

It is said one can find a little humor in any situa-
    tion,
But ours called for no laughter, for
Even getting water from the rivers was terror at
The prospect of being mauled by unseen crocodiles.
Hunger was not a problem, because we could hunt,
And the cold also, because we could make fire
By drilling sticks into sticks
Or striking together the hard stones you put in our
    bags.
The problem lay in other challenges, even tiny
    irritations, like

Being bitten by mosquitoes and other insects.
Once we lay down on a nest of red ants and sprang
    back to our feet.
On another occasion tsetse flies chased us.
A chase by bigger animals would have been more
    manageable.
Those tsetse flies may have been tiny, though bigger
    than locusts,
But their incessant *zzzz*-ing was louder than that
    from a cluster of bees.

Still, the biggest challenge was not posed by insects
  and animals.
Human wiles and wrath posed the greatest danger.
What can I tell that you don't already know?
Human-to-human cruelty is worse than that of
  beast to human.
Worse still is the cruelty among neighbors when it
  drives them
To raise machetes, spears , arrows, and clubs against
  one another.
Because of the many weeks we had been together
  and common dangers we'd fought,
We had reached a stage at which we felt like broth-
  ers and sisters,
But as we relaxed, proud of how much we had
  endured together,
Yes, just as we thought we had survived the worst,
Another group took that very moment to plan
  evil.

They claimed the women were the real root of all
  their problems,
That we had lured them from their homes by
  dreams wrought by charms,
The proof of our witchery being our actions and
  deeds, like

Our being able to endure and do things just like the
    men.
Facing danger without complaint showed that we
    were witches.
A few even cited Warigia's ways with arrows as
    more evidence of witchery:
Otherwise, how could a crawling cripple beat men,
    fully fit, in archery?
How else could a cripple shoot arrows a distance no
    man could reach?
That was pure witchery; even our beauty was an
    illusion wrought by sorcery.

If they could finish us, all their problems would
    end, some said.
But others cautioned against any such action, and
    said
The disgruntled should stop making up reasons for
    their problems.
These rejected the war between men and women,
Or any wars of us against us or between neighbors.
They swore that whoever hurt any of us women
Would face the united wrath of the other men.
Whether men or women, we were on the same
    journey.

Any injury to any of the women was injury to the
     men as well.
They would die defending us.

But we, the nine, did not wait to have the men
     defend us,
Because you brought us up able to stand up for
     ourselves.
And before the evil ones could reach their weapons,
We nine had already sprung up and climbed up
     some trees,
The way we have always done, though in play, since
     we were children.
We rained arrows near their feet, more to warn
     than hurt them.
The evil ones took to their heels and disappeared in
     the forests,
Crying out, "Witches! Witches! They have be-
     witched us."

Mwīthaga talked to those remaining, saying that
Whoever wanted to go back, better do so in peace;
That nobody'd been forced to leave home to pursue
     unknown beauty;
That there were also beautiful ones where they
     came from,

And beautiful ones will always be born in many
    places.
She reminded us of the saying from our mother,
    that
Blood must not be spilled over matters of love.
We waited to see if others would also leave, but
None rose to follow the ones who had quit.


Wanjikū reminded us that every good thing is born
    of challenges, that
Problems always trigger strong disagreements on
    causes and solutions,
But talking about the problems is the best way to
    heal differences.
Waithīra also tried to lift our hearts with words of
    hope, saying that
A task remains a task only when it has not been
    done, that starting a task
And enduring the challenges are good, but com-
    pleting it, should be our guide.
Reminding us that joy drives sorrow away,
Wangūi sang about love and understanding and
    being open to one another.
We joined in the singing; we felt better, and we
    resumed our journey.

·   ·   ·

After months of travel, we lost count of the days,
But finally we came to the bottom of the mountain.
It was more than a mountain; it scraped the
    heavens.
Of the hundred with whom we'd begun the
    journey,
Only we thirty were left.
We ululated and whistled and sang.
Some went out to hunt antelopes for food.
Others went about collecting firewood.
Yet others gathered berries in the forest.

As it was now our tradition, there was no saying
    this is men's or women's work.
We did tasks according to ability and necessity and
    inclination.
There, at the foot of the mountain, we prepared a
    big feast.
We made sure the meat roasted just right;
The smoke rose toward the mountaintop;
We ate, we sang, we danced.
Finally we lay on the ground and counted the stars.
We stayed there for a few days
To rest the body before we climbed up the moun-
    tain.

. . .

We told stories till there were no more stories to
 tell.
We sang till there were no more songs to sing.
Wangarĩ claimed that she could ride a leopard,
And this ignited other claims.
Wambũi said if Wangarĩ did so, then she would
 ride a zebra and race her.
Wanjikũ said she would join the race on a giraffe.
There rose arguments as to which was fastest, all
 saying,
"Let's see a race between leopard, zebra, and gi-
 raffe."


Wangarĩ, Wambũi, and Wanjikũ went for their
 racing animals.
Really it was a matter of picking the nearest,
Because there were plenty of each animal in the bush.
They then agreed on the starting point for the race.
We didn't worry, because we have lived with ani-
 mals,
And we have learned to talk with them.
We have also learned their likes and dislikes.
Still, some of us thought our sisters were just play-
 ing,
But suddenly the play became sheer amazement.

. . .

We sighted a giraffe speeding along the prairie
Closely followed by a zebra
Closely followed by a leopard.
We couldn't see the riders clearly because,
Given the distance, the rider and the ridden were
    indistinguishable.
Then, as we watched the scene, the riders came into
    view.
Wanjikũ clung to the neck of the giraffe,
Wambũi close behind on a zebra,
With Wangarĩ on top of a leopard, chasing them.

But when the animals sighted us cheering, they got
    the fright
And suddenly flung the three riders to the ground.
Riderless, the animals ran until they vanished from
    view.
Fearing the worst, we ran to the scene of the fall.
The riders were busy brushing off grass and checking
    their bodies,
And when it was clear they were not hurt, they start-
    ed laughing out loud.
We laughed too and asked them what happened,
Some of the men wondering aloud
What charms they'd used to tame animals of the wild.

· · ·

The man who once pulled out the arrows for Wari-
  gia
Bragged loudly about animal racing in his home
  region.
He claimed that in his area they raced while riding
  lions.
Some doubted him, and we started arguing about it.
Then he said he would ride a lion just to show us he
  could.
Another man claimed that where he came from,
  they rode rhinos.
When it came to speed, he asserted, a lion was no
  match for the rhino.
Again a dispute arose as to which was faster.
The two left to look for a lion and a rhino to ride.

The rest told stories of the animals in their home
  regions.
They measured manhood by wresting down fero-
  cious animals.
Others said one should measure one's manhood
  against another man.
Claims and counterclaims about ways of measuring
  manhood erupted.
Suddenly we saw a lion and a rhino in a tight race.

Grass flew behind them, but when the animals saw
   us cheering,
They became frightened and took flight in different
   directions.
The rhino rider fell off and rolled on the grass.
The rhino ran away and disappeared into the bush.

The lion rider met a different fate.
The animal turned, opened its mouth, and bared its
   teeth.
We shouted and screamed and raised our spears.
This may have startled the lion, and it ran away,
But not before it had scratched his arm; blood
   trickled down.
Once again, Wanjikũ dashed into the bush.
She came back with green leaves and strings and
   tied the wound.
The victim was smiling as if being wounded by a
   lion was an everyday thing.
If he'd had a spear in hand, he would have plunged
   it into the lion's mouth.
We nicknamed him Kĩhara, the scarred one.

And then we saw a large herd of elephants.
We agreed to try to ride them; they were more
   peaceful.

We went for it—each one, one elephant.
We, the elephant riders, circled each other,
While they ate grass, ignoring our weight on them.
Then some suggested we try to race, but
The elephants did not cooperate, and we got off
    their backs.
We laughed, and the laughter helped relax our
    bodies, which
Seemed to signal that playtime was over, that we
    should resume our journey.

Climbing up the mountain was another challenge.
It called for a healthy body and a strong will.
Matters did not go as smoothly as we had hoped.
After a while, some started asking if we'd ever get
    to the top.
Others said the mountain had no discernible end.
Yet others: "My heart says yes, but my body is say-
    ing no."
We did not try to pressure anybody to continue in
    the journey,
Or judge anybody who wanted to give up.
Those who lost heart to continue just turned back.

The remainder resolved to take it a step at a time.
If we need to rest, we rest.

If we need to continue, we continue.
Step after step will take us to the top;
There is no power stronger than the power of hope.
We made steady progress, up the mountain, and
Twenty-nine finally reached the top,
But the cold that hit us froze our jubilation, for
Though the heart was willing, the body was freez-
    ing.

Some declared they were not going to wait to die of
    cold.
They did not look back; they returned the way they
    had come.
A small group of men and the nine remained reso-
    lute.
We scooped some of the white moon and put it into
    the gourds.
Our fingers were freezing as if bitten by the whiteness.
When about to start the journey down the moun-
    tain,
We heard steps behind us.
One of those who had just left us had now come
    back to us.
He said that his heart told him he could not go
    back without Warigia.
He would return with us.

He was the one we had named Kīhara, after he was
   mauled by the lion.
We welcomed him back, such a beautiful young
   man.
We climbed down together, and we came to some
   lakes.
We filled our gourds with the holy water, thus mix-
   ing it with the moon.
And suddenly we realized what we had achieved.
"Victory! Victory!" we shouted together.
Wangūi started to sing; we joined in.
Our voices paid tribute to the beauty of the land
   around us.

# 10

## The Ogre and the Cure-All Hair

Njeri suggested we take different routes to circum-
vent the crocodile rivers.
After a few days, we entered a forest so thick that
We could not tell day from night and it was fatigue
that forced us to rest.
We made fire, and, as was our habit, we took turns
for rest and guard duty.
Some stayed awake as watchmen while the rest of
us slept.
Wanjirū interrupted our sleep; human screams had
awoken her.
She had even seen, or thought she had, a big tongue
snatch our guards,
But she couldn't tell if it was a nightmare or not.
We stared at one another in terror, for indeed
We couldn't see any of the three guards.
We said we should wait until dawn to look for
them.
Then Waithīra heard some steps heading toward us.
We struck the hard stones together, as you taught
us, and

Waited for the sound echo to help us locate the
    source of the steps
Or even estimate the size of the thing that made
    them.
But no echo came back.

Suddenly we heard a voice loud as thunder:
"This forest is ogreland! Go back to where you
    came from."
The thundering voice shook the forest. And yet
We still could not tell the direction it came from.
We pointed spears and arrows in all directions.
Wanjirū offered to talk to it so that, as it answered,
    we would estimate its location.
"Who are you? A bodiless voice?
Are you a human, a bad spirit, or a good spirit?"
"I am Mwengeca, king of ogres," the bodiless voice
    answered.

We looked blindly around at each other in the
    dark: The Mwengeca you told us about?
The one with the hair that could give power back to
    Warigia's legs?
"How can we tell that you really are the Mwenge-
    ca?" Wanjirū asked,
"Because right now we can't even see you."

"My body cannot be seen with human eyes," the
    ogre said.
"It is impossible for you to know where I am,
    whether far or near.
My tongue is also my eye and mouth.
It shines like lightning and creates a path of light in
    the dark.
It lengthens like a chameleon's reaching out for a
    fly.
It sees all and reaches all the corners of my forest.

"My hair cures all. Call it the cure-all,
For there is no wound it cannot heal.
Is that why you come to my forest?
To steal my cure-all?
Why do you want to end illnesses on earth?"
"We have no wounds in the heart or body for you
    to cure," said Wanjirū.
"Besides, we can cure ourselves. You are not the
    only know-it-all."
"You, the talkative dame, are the one I have always
    looked for," said Mwengeca.
"Smooth-tongued Wanjirū, join me and together
    we rule my Forest Kingdom."

Wanjirū's group shouted back in unison:

"A greedy heart has no cure but a knife in the
    heart."
Spears raised, some of them made as if to move, but
Wanjirū restrained them, saying, "Let the head lead
    the heart."
Hurry hurry hardly ever gets things right.
What they sought from this ogre called for a wily
    mind.
She had not even finished, when out came a wide
    red tongue.


Before we had recovered from the shock, the tongue
    caught three other men,
Tying them together and pulling the human bundle
    to its hiding place.
At first their cries to us and Wanjirū for help were
    loud, but
The sounds kept on fading and then suddenly came
    to an end.
We knew, without seeing it, that the ogre had swal-
    lowed the men.
Eerie silence fell upon the entire forest; our hearts
    grew cold,
And our bodies shook like reeds in the wind.
"We don't have the luxury of trembling with ter-
    ror," Wanjirū said and

Quickly jumped and hid behind a tree at the same
    time,
Shouting to us to hide behind the nearest tree but
Making sure to leave an imaginary space in the
    middle.
We had to be ready with our bows and arrows and
    spears
So that when she called out *"Now!"* we would all
    attack the tongue, and
Whoever found an opportunity would pull out the
    hair in the middle of it.
After giving us sufficient time to hide behind trees,
Wanjirū hurled the same insult her group had
    earlier shouted:
"A greedy heart has no other cure but a spear in the
    heart."

We who grew up with Wanjirū knew her heart was
    bleeding tears.
But one could not tell this by her strong, arrogant,
    defiant tongue.
The invisible ogre was very angry at fearless
    Wanjirū.
At once it sent its tongue in her direction,
But before it could ensnare her, she deftly moved
    aside.

The long wide tongue tied itself around the tree.
*"Now!"* Wanjirũ shouted.
Our arrows pinned the tongue to the tree.
Wanjirũ shot hers at the eye at the tongue's end.


Kĩhara quickly jumped onto the tongue,
Which was as wide as a path, and
Walked about on it looking for the magical hair.
He bounced up and down on the elastic tongue.
The ogre couldn't see him because its eye had been
    pierced.
But the moment Kĩhara pulled out the hair,
Mwengeca let out a blood-curdling scream.
His voice sounded like thunder,
And a redness, like lightning, kept on flashing.


Then Mwengeca roared again, and
He pulled back its tongue with all his strength.
He was able to free it, but it was torn into nine
    straps,
And now the ogre had no eye, because it had been
    pierced.
Wanjirũ told us she'd hatched the plan of action
The moment the ogre ensnared the second group of
    men.

"Oh, but where is the hair," Wanjirū asked, as she
    recalled the mission.

Kīhara raised his hand, his eyes bright with joy:

"For Warigia!" he shouted in a tone that said he
    alone would carry it back.

11

# The Ogre of Endless Darkness

We resumed our journey and, for a time, did not
    encounter any surprises.

But we remained alert so as not to be trapped by
    Mwengeca, for

Although we had pierced his eye and plucked out
    the magical hair,

We had not hurt his body, because we couldn't see it.

His body might have been healed and his sight
    restored.

At night we took turns to sleep and guard.

The watch people formed a circle around the sleep-
    ing ones.

We would then change places, those formerly asleep
    now forming the circle.

But even so, it was difficult to find sound sleep.


Another night, soon after organizing ourselves to
    sleep,

We heard some steps heading our way.

We looked about us, but what we saw was a dark-
    ness so deep,

It made the rest of darkness, by contrast, appear as
   daylight.
Darkness darker than darkness? What was this?
On further scrutiny, we saw the darkness take a
   human shape,
But we could not make out its actual height and
   width.
Before we could recover from our stupor and figure
   out what to do,
We heard a voice thunder out across the land.

"I am *TheDarknessDarkerThanDarkness*!
I make clean hearts darker than darkness by
Leading them into paths of darkness and leaving
   them there.
My darkness can never be undarkened.
My darkness is in the eternal service to the king of
   ogres.
From what I grab for him, I make sure to take my
   share first.
My motto: 'Grab for self before grabbing for anoth-
   er self.'
What's lodged in one's tummy is invisible to others.

"If you don't want me to plunge you into darkness
   darker than darkness,

Hand over Wangarī to me, and I will let the rest go."

Just as the men were about to throw spears into the
  darkness,

Mwīthaga stopped them. "Have you not learned
  much from our experiences?

You don't strike unless you can clearly see what you
  are aiming at."

Some in her group ignored her admonition, saying,

"True, but we can see this one with the eyes of men,"
  and

Holding their spears firmly, they plunged into the
  darkness.

The darkness sucked in the ones in the lead immedi-
  ately.

Then we heard the sound of heads being crushed.

The screams of the victims went straight into our
  hearts.

The others stopped themselves in time and came back
  to us.

Oh! We never saw those sucked in by the dark alive
  again.

The darkness laughed derisively but loudly enough for
  us to hear.

It will swallow us all as it did our comrades, it
  bragged.

And indeed the shadowy menace started edging
　　toward us,
Demanding we surrender Wangarī to the darkly
　　dark darkness.

And Wangarī? You should have seen her.
She was trembling with rage and proud defiance,
And she shouted her challenge back into the dark-
　　ness,
Her words echoing through the entire forest.
"My name is Wangarī, and I have the bright eyes of
　　a leopard.
Mine can clear any darkness like the sun in the day
　　or the moon at night.
I dare you to come near me, and I will clear you
　　with the light of a leopard's eyes."
The ogre of endless darkness stopped advancing,
As if the word "light" was itself a spear or an arrow
　　aimed at its heart.

Wangarī realized something and acted on it imme-
　　diately.
She clashed the stones together to generate fire, and
　　she lit up a firebrand.
When the darkness saw the light, it screamed and
　　started retreating ignominiously.

We others also made fire, and with our flaming
    bundles, we chased the darkness.
Every time the ogre saw the light advancing toward
    it,
It speeded its retreat, bending or uprooting
Trees and plants, before it finally vanished.
We added more wood to the fire for a bonfire.

The redness of sun rising at dawn found us there,
And we, despite our sorrow, welcomed the sun with
    a song:

*Sun, the ruler of the universe,*
*Without you there is no light.*
*Without you there is no heat.*

*The sun keeps all animals warm.*
*The sun keeps all plants warm.*
*The sun keeps men, women, and children warm.*

We found the bodies of the three men dead under
    a tree,
Their heads split; the ogre had hit them against the
    tree.

# 12

# The Ogre That Fumed Fire and Fury

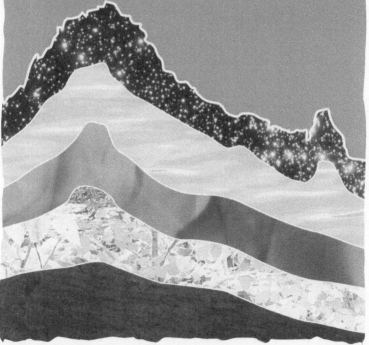

Mwengeca and the Ogre of Darkness left us with
  unanswered questions.
Had Mwengeca turned himself into the Ogre of
  Darkness,
Perhaps as vengeance for having lost his tongue and
  eye?
Others said no, the two were different types of
  ogres.
An ogre was an ogre, no matter their names, some
  asserted.
The debate helped us take our thoughts away from
  sorrow,
While also keeping our minds occupied.
Now we traveled only by the light of day.
At night we made a bonfire, talked, and took turns
  to sleep.

A few days without a mishap—peace returned to
  our hearts.
But one morning, about to resume our journey,
We heard weird sounds behind us.

We took to our heels, then stopped and
Looked back to find out what was behind us.
A strange apparition met our eyes:
Was it human, an animal, or what?
A creature with three legs and three arms?
The creature grabbed the burning fire and swal-
	lowed it.

More inexplicable wonders followed.
It breathed out flames from its mouths and
	nose.
The flames incinerated the bush and the plants
	around it.
Once again we took to our heels: running away in
	defense of self is not cowardice.
The three-legged ogre pursued us, shouting brags
	and threats:
"I am the burner that burns up even those that defy
	other fires.
I burn everything in my way, be it near or far from
	me."
No matter how fast we ran, it kept up the pursuit,
	breathing out smoke and fire,
Demanding we surrender Mwīthaga to it as a price
	to let us go.

Though we did not see it clearly because
It was surrounded by smoke and flames,
We knew that its three legs and arms hampered its
    movement,
For the limbs were not well coordinated.
But it could spit out noisy flames quite far,
And while we panted with fatigue, it never seemed
    to tire.
From an early age, you taught us to walk and
    run.
But some of the young men were not used to run-
    ning like us,
So when they breathed, their lungs screamed
    fatigue.

After some distance, we heard the men in the very
    rear
Cry out with a pain that went to our hearts and
    heads.
We took it that the flames had reached them.
Our pain was deepened by our knowing that we
    could not stop to help them.
Mwīthaga suggested we climb up a mugumo fig
    tree, for
We couldn't outrun an ogre that never tired.
The fig tree was big and tall, with many branches.

The three-legged creature stopped at the bottom of
    the tree.
And its flames did not reach us; the ogre seemed
    unable to throw them high.

From her position on the branch above, Mwīthaga
    started mocking the creature:
They call me Mwīthaga, also Nyambura, who sings;

*Rain rain down.*
*I will give you*
*The ugly one*
*With three legs*
*And three arms*
*Dry like stones.*
*It can't run.*
*It can't lift.*
*It can't drink.*
*Rain pour down.*

When it heard this, it seemed to hesitate as if in
    fear,
And this hesitancy taught Mwīthaga something.
She poured out the mountain water from her
    gourd,

Chanting incantations to charm the rain.
And it started raining.
The leaves amplified the sound of rain.
The Ogre of Fire and Fury took to its heels
And ran away screaming till it vanished in the
    distance.
And we never saw or heard of it again.

# 13

# The Ogre That Shat Without Stopping

We didn't get far without Mwengeca flinging other
    challenges,
But that for every challenge we found an answer.
As you always taught us, to every closure, there's a
    disclosure.

The Ogre of Endless Tears caught us as we
    mourned our recent loss.
Its tears flowed down from its eyes like water from
    a pipe,
Triggering our own tears, which now flowed down
    without stopping,
But when it demanded Wambūi for it to clear our
    tears, we knew
It wanted sorrow to drown hope.
We shall not lose hope as intended by the enemy,
    we resolved.
We started laughing, and this chased away the Ogre
    of Endless Tears.
Hope and expectations came back to us,
And we resumed our journey with renewed vigor.

The Ogre of Floods chased us, throwing waves and
    wet dirt at us.
So we ran as fast as we could and climbed up a hill
    to the top.
When it failed to climb the hill, the ogre receded,
    defeated.

The Ogre That Shat Without Stopping created
    mountains of shit.
The air around smelled of pure rot.
The leaves of plants and trees looked limp.
Birds fell down dying;
Others left their nests and fled the area.
Insects were dying, while others tried to move away.
We feared that the rot might pollute the rivers.
Polluting air and water is poisoning life.
We chased the ogre with the sweet smell of fresh
    flowers.

The most menacing—that is,
If there was an ogre that could out-evil the others,
It was the Bloodthirsty Ogre, for it demanded
    blood from us,
Even trying to persuade us that it was making us a
    good offer

Because it wanted only our blood, not our flesh.
It would just suck the blood from the veins and
    leave the body intact.
We lured it into a deep hole into which it fell.
We left it there, crying out, "Please help me out.
If you leave me here, I will die for lack of blood."

Finally we came to a river flowing with clean water.
    What a joy!
The river marked the boundary between Mwenge-
    ca's forest,
And the forest on the other side of the river, whose
    owner we did not know.
Some of the men claimed it looked wider than all
    the rivers they had ever crossed.
We walked up and down the banks, looking for the
    narrowest crossing point.
We carefully checked for signs of crocodiles in the
    reeds.
And then, as soon as we found a good spot from
    where to swim across,
And rejoicing that we were about to leave the forest
    of ogres,
We heard a deep voice from across the river.

14

The
Ogres
with Bags
That Never
Filled
Up

I am the Squint-Eyed Ogre, who smashes people's
    heads into pieces,
The ogre who makes people do as he says whether
    they like it or not,
The ogre who makes men swallow dirt whether
    they like it or not.
Wairimũ, I have come for you to make you the
    beloved wife of the ogres.
We looked up across the waterfall and saw a big
    fellow looming over the waters,
And we knew it was he who was vomiting out the
    menacing words.
His hair fell over his body and the leather bag he
    carried.
He was an ogre just like those under Mwengeca's
    rule,
Or those you always told us about in our evenings
    of storytelling.

What distinguished this from Mwengeca's clan was
    the eyes.

This had only one eye on its forehead, and it shone
    bright like a sun's ray.
When we did not answer back, it roared thunder:
"Wairimũ, beloved, come home to the ogres to cook
    for them."
We should have been immune to wonders, but still
    we froze with terror,
Unable to decide whether to take flight or fight
    back.
We felt trapped between the terror behind us and
    the terror in front, for
Mwengeca and his band of blood-drinking ogres lay
    behind us, and
In front, across the river, stood the One-Eyed Ogre.
In the midst of our indecision, Wanjikũ spoke out:
"Hesitation in self-defense is not a show of cowardice.
We don't look for war, but
If it is visited on us, we can't just give in."
We all agreed with her.
We ran down the banks of the river,
But just as we thought we had lost the ogre,
We saw it on the other side of the river.
We ran back up the river the way we'd come,
But then we saw it facing us on the other side of the
    river.

      . . .

Wairimū was furious and shouted:

"They call me Wairimū and not the beloved of any
      ogre.

I don't want to hear your foolishness, or I will beat
      it out of you."

We all swore that no matter how many they were,

The ogres of this world were never again going to
      make us run away,

Because the more we ran away from them or soft-
      ened them with bribes,

The more they felt emboldened and panted for more.

The ogre was angry at Wairimū's defiance and
      swore that

If we did not give him whom it wanted, it would
      store us all in its bag.


"It looks as if you don't know me," it shouted, "so let
      me tell you who I am.

They call me the Squint-Eyed Ogre, but actually,
      my one eye sees far.

The Ogre of the Big Bag is also my name, because
      my bag never fills up."

And as soon as he said so, he bent down near the
      falls, and lo,

The river started flowing into its bag, and it did not
      get full.

The whole river, including the falls, flowed into the
  bag,
And it never got full.
When we saw dry earth where the river had been,
We decided to cross the dry valley and take the
  fight to the ogre.

More wonders! He let out the water from the leath-
  er bag.
The river resumed; if we had crossed, we would
  have been caught in the middle.
"Give me Wairimū, the beloved of ogres. I'll take
  her to the ogres' palace,
And the rest of you will be free to go in peace."

"I don't want to hear your foolishness," Wairimū
  shouted back.
"My name is Wairimū, and I have nothing to do
  with ogres.
I am the daughter of Gīkūyū and Mūmbi.
I am not lazy like you.
I eat what I grow;
I drink the water I draw;
I live in a house I have built.
I don't want to hear your foolishness,
Or I will beat it out of you."

Just then an antelope and a gazelle passed by.
The ogre snatched them one after the other;
He put them in the bag that never gets full.
He startled us with many other wonders, like
Swallowing trees, soil, all of them into his bag,
All the time threatening us that,
If we refused to give up Wairimũ,
We would end up in the bag that never filled up.
Defiantly, Wairimũ threatened to tear open the
    ogre's big tummy,
And free all the people's property it had swal-
    lowed.

And our young men were roaring with defiant rage.
One of them volunteered to go and fight it alone.
He grabbed his spear and, with all his might, threw
    it across the river.
We were all amazed, because
The ogre caught the spear in the air with its hand.
It broke it into pieces and put them in the bag.
Three other men threw theirs at the same time.
The ogre grabbed them in the air, broke them into
    pieces,
And threw them into the bag that never got full.

Another two went behind the group and
Then crawled through bush down the riverside.
The rest distracted the ogre with endless provoca-
tive questions
Just to buy the young men time to find a good point
from which to cross.
Their aim was to approach the ogre from behind
and pierce it with spears,
But when eventually they crossed and threw their
spears at its back,
The ogre didn't even turn round but grabbed the
spears in midair.
It broke them to pieces and put them into the bag
that never filled up,
Laughing derisively, its one eye still fixed on us.

It did the same with their arrows:
Grab, break, and put them in the bag.
It was then we understood it had another eye at the
back.
Wairimū felt anger mount inside her.
She grabbed a spear from the man next to her, and
She threw it with all her might,
It whistled in the air,
It passed above the head of the ogre,
But the ogre did not even try to catch it.

Wairimũ then said it was her turn to tackle the ogre.

We begged her not to do anything by herself, alone,

Even if it meant us perishing together.

"This is my fight with these ogres," Wairimũ said.

"No," we said, "the fight against ogres is not one person's fight;

And the power of four people united is far more effective

Than that of eight people as individuals.

Once it swallows you, it will do the same with us,

One by one, store us in the bag that never fills up."

Wairimũ told us not to worry.

She urged us to keep hurling stones at the ogre without stopping.

With her bow and arrow ready and the quiver on her back,

Wairimũ crept through the bush and climbed up a tree.

Soon afterward we heard the ogre scream with pain,

Its thundering voice shaking the ground on which we stood.

Arrow after arrow found their mark into the head
     of the ogre.
And then we saw it take to its heels,
Arrows sticking from its head like the quills of a
     hedgehog.

Wairimũ came down. She told us she got the idea
     when she first threw a spear at it.
It was then that she realized the ogre could see only
     in front or back.
It could not turn its neck up
Or bend its neck to look down
Or even look from side to side.
Now we went down the river and found a good spot
     from which to cross.
We reunited with the two brave young men who
     had crossed earlier,
And all of us together rejoiced, for none of us was
     hurt.
We sang in praise of Wairimũ and the brave men.

In the midst of our joy and celebration of
     Wairimũ,
We found ourselves surrounded by eight other
     ogres,

Very angry that we had shot their leader with
    arrows.
They said in unison that their bags never get full.
They threatened to swallow us and the soil and the
    air and the water—
Because their bags never can get full, they repeated
    together.
But now we didn't get too frightened because we
    knew their weakness.
This time we asked Wairimū and others to keep
    them distracted,
And the others climbed up trees, each taking on
    one of the ogres.

The ogres did as their chief had earlier.
They took to their heels screaming,
But still swearing by their bags that could never get
    full.
We could tell that one of them was a baby ogre
    because
It was crying out in a very thin voice,
"My parent, I am not hurt, and as much as my
    name is Manga
I will surely give rise to more ogres," it asserted as
    it followed his progenitor,

Which, panting, shouted back, "That's spoken like
    my offspring! Send them an ogre culture."
The property of the unvigilant will always prop up
    the clan of ogres.

15

# The Hyena and the Vulture

We encountered so many wonders that
Even now, as I recount these stories,
I feel I am talking about dreams, or
Nightmares that make one sweat on waking.

Once we saw a giant forest in front of us.
The trees bore beautiful flowers of all colors,
But when we approached it hoping to pick some,
The entire forest disappeared into the earth, but
After we crossed the now treeless area and looked
    back,
The entire forest had emerged back from the earth.

Another time we came to the banks of a river,
We stopped, transfixed by the sight before us.
An ogre removed its leg, but no blood came out.
It washed the leg in the waters.
Then the ogre lay it on the grass to dry.

It did the same with the other leg.
Then it turned to its noses and ears,

All the limbs one by one
Including the eyes, finally,
Plucking, washing them, and putting them on the
   grass to dry.

The two eyes began to play about;
Then they chased each other,
Rolling in our direction, but
When they saw us, they cried out
And started rolling back.

On hearing the scream, the other limbs
Jumped up one by one and
Reunited with the rest of the body.
The eyes were still screaming.
Two of our men shot the eyes, and we took to our
   heels.

Later we encountered two more ogres, who,
When they saw us, started running away.
We chased them, but then one of them changed
   into a vulture,
The other into a big hyena, and both followed us,
The vulture in the sky and the hyena stealthily
   through the bushes.

   . . .

We knew they were waiting for any one of us to tire
    and collapse;
They would then fall to the carcass for their food of
    the day.
We decided to shoot down a gazelle.
The vulture, its talons out, raced the hyena to the
    carcass.
And that was how we escaped the vulture and the
    hyena.

16

# Ogres
# in
# White
# Masks

Finally we left the forest of the ogres with bags that
   never got full.
We came to grass plains populated by herds of
   different animals.
There were those that ate grass and leaves—
Giraffes, gazelles, zebras, antelopes, buffalo;
Those, like the family of lions, that preyed on other
   animals;
And varieties of flying birds and partridges and
   ostriches.
The wealth of wildlife reminding us of at the foot-
   hills of the mountain,
Except that now we were on our way back to Gath-
   anga.
Suddenly another wonder sprang up before us.
I can't remember who first spotted him, but

He was extremely well built, a beauty the color of
   chalk.
The entire body, together with the clothes, was
   chalk white.

His hair—long, straight, and soft-looking—fell on
his back and shoulders.
It was also chalky, whiter than the whiteness of an
ostrich.
But let the rays of the setting sun fall on his body
and clothes,
And they shone with more than the seven colors of
the rainbow.
And then he whistled at us.
I cannot tell what madness got to us, the nine, all at
the same time, but
Disputes erupted among us, each claiming he was
the one her heart desired.

Wanjikū was the first to come to her senses, and she
talked to us:
"Don't despise the beads you are wearing for the
ones worn by another.
Don't give up the four in your hand for the eight in
the hands of another.
Since when does chalk beauty beat black beauty?
How can we abandon the men with whom we have
suffered
For somebody we don't even know?
Chalk?

Have we forgotten the admonition from Mother
    Mũmbi?
Let our eyes return to those whose character has
    been proven by deeds."

Our men were looking at the other side of the
    plains,
Where stood a well-built woman with the body of
    chalk.
Her hair was also soft, long, straight.
Like that of the chalk man, it fell on her back; it
    was as if they were twins.
When a breeze made some hair cover her eyes, she
    deftly pushed it aside with
Her chalked fingers and nails, hands that looked as
    if they had never touched soil.
She sang a song that seemed to make our men
    crazy,
And they began to quarrel over her, just as we had
    done over her twin.
Our men had forgotten all that they had endured
    in search of black beauty.

Kĩhara was the only one who resisted the new
    shining object—

Yes, the same man who once pulled out the arrows
    for Warigia,
The same who was once scratched by a lion,
The same who plucked the cure-all hair from
    Mwengeca's tongue,
The same who refused to part with it and claimed
    the trophy for Warigia.
He proclaimed, loud and clear, that his heart chose
    his own long ago,
That even when his chosen one was not here in body,
His heart was firmly anchored in Warigia's, and
It was not about to be blown away by chalked
    beauty.

The men were deep in disputes about their clashing
    claims,
Each saying that he was the first to spot her,
Or claiming that the song she sang was aimed at
    him alone.
Then there came some wind, so strong it almost
    blew off our skirts.
The wind revealed a horror to beat all the previous
    wonders.
The hair of the chalked ones was the first to be
    blown off,
Leaving their heads bare.

Heads, did I say? No, skulls.
Wait! Not just the skulls for heads!

Their entire bodies were skeletons of bones, which
Had worn the masks of human body and hair.
Exposed, the two skeletons ran wildly across the
    plains.
Even the animals retreated at the frightening sight
    and sound,
For the skeletons were making jarring noises.
Finally the skeletons disappeared in the forest of
    the ogres.
We stared at each other in wonder, amazement, and
    relief.
We said thank you to Wanjikū and Kīhara for
    standing firm;
They had prevented us from becoming slaves of
    ogres in chalky masks.

# 17

# The Hair That Cures All Illnesses

We were ninety-nine when we left home, an imma-
    ture lot,
Hope and doubt fighting for dominance in our
    hearts.
When danger appeared, doubt deepened, but
Hope said no to the whispers of doubt, and
Expectations added strength to hope.
We faced many trials in our journey,
Which turned out to be a test of heart and body.
You cannot be without trying to be.
We were nineteen when we came back, a mature
    lot,

For we had seen sorrow and joy fight in our hearts,
Sorrow for those who didn't make it,
Some eaten by crocodiles,
Others victims of despair, allowing pessimism to
    rein in hope,
And others, victims of the various ogres.
What gave us joy was the moon we collected from
    the mountaintop,

Together with the water drawn from the lake up
    there,
Evidence that we did indeed get to the top of the
    Mountain of the Moon,
That indeed we had stepped in your footsteps and

Walked the walk you once walked,
Drunk from the calabash you once drank from,
And sung the song you once sang.
We came back nineteen in all, ever vigilant,
And now we know that ogres don't dwell in tales
    alone
And that, though different in types and colors, all are
    human-eaters.
Their challenges taught us that without continuous
    vigilance, we shall fall.
Our biggest trophy of victory was Mwengeca's hair.

Gĩkũyũ poured a little libation and called for silence.
"The power that brought you back is the same that
    once brought us here.
Your journey is blessed, and we are grateful that,
Even without the hair that cures all, Warigia's legs
    have regained power."
Just at that moment, Warigia emerged carrying an
    antelope on her shoulder.

She'd gone out to hunt alone, Mũmbi told them,
    and assured them that
They would no longer have to worry for Warigia,
    that life was full of wonders.
After they left for the mountain, Warigia had start-
    ed crawling down to the river
To meet with the spirit of her lover, she said,
Sure that he would come back the way he had gone,
    by the river.
She would sit on a rock by the riverside and dip her
    legs in the water.
Other times she would lie on the rocks and let the
    water flow all over her.

One day, we heard thunder and saw lightning such
    as we had never seen before,
It felt as if heaven and earth were breaking apart at
    the same moment.
Then, as abruptly, the thunder and the lightning
    ceased.

We looked at one another: "Oh, where is our
    daughter? Has fate come for her?"
Your father and I left for the river, hurrying as if
    going to war.

We met Warigia on her way home, walking firmly
    on her two beautiful legs.

"When did this miracle happen?" we asked in uni-
    son. "Was it soon after we left?"

"No, you had been away for a number weeks, like
    one season gone," Gĩkũyũ said.

The group kept silent but started calculating, then
    stared at one another.

The miracle coincided with the moment Kĩhara
    uprooted Mwengeca's hair.

# 18

# Betrothal

Wanjirū and her man walked in step, slowly, hold-
    ing the gourd together.
They placed it at the feet of Gīkūyū and Mūmbi.
The moonwhite had long turned to water, and only
    a few drops were left.
Gīkūyū dipped his fly whisk into the pot and sprin-
    kled blessings over them.
"May this water wash away all impurities in the
    path of your lives together."

"Peace! May the Giver Supreme bless you," said
    Mūmbi.
She did the same, dipped a fly whisk in the pot, and
    sprinkled blessings over them.
"Peace! May the Giver Supreme clear ogres from all
    your paths.
Now is the time for the lover and the loved to love
    in heart and body.
May many children come out of this union of
    hearts, to play on these grounds."

177

The others went through similar rites of parental
    blessings—
All of them, that is, except Warigia and her man,
The man once scarred by a lion, the man whom
    they named Kīhara,
The man who plucked the cure-all hair from
    Mwengeca's tongue.
They didn't have a gourd, for Warigia had not
    joined the expedition.

Warigia ran into her mother's hut.
She came back carrying a pot full of water.
Her man joined her; they lifted it together, and
They placed it at the feet of Gīkūyū and Mūmbi.
"I, Warigia, who stayed behind to take care of you,
    now say:

"Kīhara is the one my heart chose at the moment of
    our first encounter.
And there was nothing that would have happened,
    during the journey or after,
That would have made my heart turn to another.
Water is water! The river where I drew this water
    has origins in the same mountain,
So bless us with this water; it's holy to me, for it
    helped heal my legs."

Gĩkũyũ welcomed all the love pairs. The men were
   no longer strangers to the house.
They had declared their intentions for the future,
   then sought and got blessings.
"Mũmbi and her daughters will now go back to the
   mother's hut as before,
But the men will now go to their huts named after
   their chosen ones.
We shall begin marriage ceremonies after nine
   days."

# 19

## Adoption and Clan Names

After the requisite nine days were over,
Gĩkũyũ and Mũmbi called the pairs together,
For the would-be grooms to be born again,
"So we can truly firm up our oneness," Gĩkũyũ said,
"And ensure that the clans you will bear will have
    names."

"Wanjirũ and Njirũ
Be born again as Njirũ, for
Your beloved is Wanjirũ. Together,
May your hard work yield plenty.
May blessings pour upon you, the Njirũs, and give
    you
The power to build a new home,
Home of the Njirũs,
From which to build the House of the Njirũs,
And the houses of Njirũs to build the clan of Njirũs
And the clan of Njirũs help build the nation."

All the other pairs went through a similar rite.
These are the origins of the names of the nine clans:

Wambũi and Mbũi, for the Mbũi clan;
Wanjikũ and Njikũ, for the Njikũ clan;
Wangũi and Ngũi, for the Thiegeni clan;
Waithĩra and Ngeci, for the Ngeci clan;
Njeri and Cera, for the Cera clan;
Nyambura and Mwĩthaga, for the Ethaga clan;
Wairimũ and Gathiigia, for the Gathiigia clan;
Wangarĩ and Ngarĩ, for the Ngarĩ clan; and
Warigia and Mũyũ, for the Mũyũ clan.

## 20

# The First Marriage

The wedding of Wanjirū and Njirū was the first
    marital ceremony.
The bride woke up early and dressed in a long soft
    leather skirt,
Trimmed at the edges with shells and beads.
Multicolored bead necklaces hung loose over the
    dress,
The bunched beads and earrings swinging slightly
    in rhythm with her walk.
Njirū, the bridegroom, was also in leather wear,
Which fitted him so well it was as if he were born
    into it.
The two spent the whole morning adorning them-
    selves.

Gīkūyū and Mūmbi had woken up at first light,
    well before sunrise.
They stood in the yard, the birds chirping all
    around them.
They stood facing the mountain and sprinkled
    libation.

*Mũmbi said:*

"Water is life for humans, animals, and plants.
Water makes the mud out of which life is molded.
The sun sends rays of heat into the muddy dough,
And breathes the breath of life into the dough.
The earth drinks the water and seeds sprout."

*Gĩkũyũ said:*

"God, the Giver Supreme, we beseech you:
Banish all blemishes from any direction—
Northern, Southern, Eastern, or Western—
That may threaten to harm these lives."

*Mũmbi said:*

"With this water, bless these children,
And my grandchildren and great-grandchildren.
Bind the family together with the power of our
    people,
The past, the living, and those to come, the triad of
    life."

*Mũmbi and Gĩkũyũ together:*

Peace! Glory to the Giver, Supreme Peace.
Peace! Glory to the Giver, Supreme Peace.
Peace! Glory to the Giver, Supreme Peace.

In the afternoon, with all the other nine present,
All dressed in leather, beads, and other decorations,
And accompanied by all their intendeds,
Wanjirū and Njirū stood before Gĩkũyũ and Mũm-
    bi.

*Gĩkũyũ said:*
"This is the first matrimony in this house.
This is a ceremony to bless the beginnings of the
    House of Mũmbi.
May you increase and multiply more than the stars
    above."

*Mũmbi said:*
"The beginning of the beginning to multiply,
The beginning of more yields to come,
The beginning of a new tomorrow."

*Gĩkũyũ said:*
"Life has and has not a beginning.
Life has and has not an end.
The beginning is the end and the end is the begin-
    ning."

*Mūmbi said:*

"Yes the beginning and the end are mothers to each
  other.

The end of one phase is the beginning of another.

The end of one thing is the beginning of another.

Death of one seed is the birth of many others."

*Gĩkũyũ said:*

"A new beginning comes from the old one,

Which began from an older beginning,

And between the beginning and the end,

There are small beginnings and ends like the divisions
  on a sugarcane,

The end and the beginning giving birth to each
  other."

*Mūmbi said:*

"These things we give you to enable the beginning of a
  new life, because

You, the woman, have come from this house and you,
  the man, from another.

Together you begin a new home.

This house and that house give birth to a third house,

And so it shall always be, the relay of life."

. . .

*Gĩkũyũ said:*

"These things are gifts to escort you on your jour-
 ney of life.
Every traveler carries some supplies for the journey."

*Mũmbi said:*

"And we gift you in the name of the parents,
Those of us here present and those unable to be
 here,
From today to the future, the parents of the groom
 and those of the bride
Will contribute to the beginning of a new home,
Gifts to start the bride and groom off to a blessed
 beginning."

*Gĩkũyũ said:*

"From now on, Njirũ is my son, son-in-law.
He will call me Father, Father-in-law.
From now on your parents are four,
We two and Njirũ's two, our in-laws.
Your children will call me Grandfather,
And call the groom's father Grandfather.

*Mũmbi said:*

"And I, mother of the bride, Grandmother;
And the mother of groom, Grandmother.

Now Njirū is my son.
He will call me Mother,
And you'll call his mother Mother."

## Enabling the Beginning of a New Home

Two machetes, tools for cultivating land, were the
first gifts.
Then the gift of seeds for planting varieties of plant
food:
Sorghum, millet , sweet potatoes, yams, and arrow-
roots.
They were given two of each type of domestic
animal:
A heifer and a bull, a billy goat and a nanny, a ram
and a ewe.

Then they were shown their own piece of the wild
to tame:
They were to turn some of it into fields for growing
food.
The other sections were to be grazing fields.
They were given two spears and two shields,
And leather cloths with several decorations.

## Ceremony for Sharing a Bean

Wanjirū and Njirū shared a single cooked bean.
They swore to always cultivate, plant, and harvest
together,
Sharing work and duties according to ability,
And, whatever they produced, to share it with
respect.

*Gĩkũyũ said:*
"Now that you have broken beans together,
May you be blessed with good yields,
To be able to feed yourselves and your children."

Njirū, the groom, cut a piece of meat from the
shoulder blade and fed the bride.
Wanjirū, the bride, did the same and fed the
groom.

*Mũmbi said:*
"Because you have now shared a shoulder blade,
Your arms have joined together.
You will herd cattle and goats that yield milk.
Your hands are now joined together.
You cultivate fields that will yield more and more."

*Gīkūyū and Mūmbi said:*

"Husband and wife, may you together make a new
  home.

May you give us grandchildren who will give us
  great-grandchildren,

Life flowing from generation to generation."

*Gīkūyū said:*

"And the woman, who carries the flow of life,

Be it a boy or a girl, for nine months, deserves
  reverence.

Woman is the mother of life,

For she is the one who carries the womb of life.

Woman is the carrier of creation. We show her
  gratitude always."

When the gifting was over, the others escorted
  Wanjirū and Njirū,

With songs and drums, all the way to their new
  home,

The women singing the song of farewell to her
  previous bed,

The men joining and adding to harmony,

And moving in rhythm with the song.

. . .

Gĩkũyũ and Mũmbi walked around the new couple's home,
Mũmbi from the left side and Gĩkũyũ the right side,
Dipping a fly whisk in the water and sprinkling libation.
They finally met at the entrance.
Wanjirũ and Njirũ entered their new home,
With the other nine ululating.

The other matrimonies followed the same pattern,
Every nine days a ceremony.
Wangũi and Ngũi's was the ninth.
After that, it was Warigia's turn,
The nine pairs to become the Perfect Nine.

# 21

# Warigia

After another nine days, all eyes turned to Warigia
    and Kīhara—
Kīhara, who at the mountain left for home and
    then rejoined the group,
The same who sustained a scratch from a Lion,
    earning him the name Kīhara,
The same who once plucked the hair that cures all
    from Mwengeca's tongue.
They all loved him; he was one of them, as if they
    had grown up together.

They had eaten and drunk together and fought
    against ogres together.
He was the first of the men to rebuff the lure of the
    chalked ogre.
The nine loved Warigia, their baby sister.
She was the last born; they had all brought her up,
Often competing as to who would carry her on her
    back.

They fed her, bathed her, or dressed her.

They had shared in Warigia's struggles with life.
Her matrimony brought them joy, and they had
    many gifts for her,
But before Gĩkũyũ and Mũmbi began the ceremo-
    ny of blessings,
Kĩhara, the groom, asked to say a few words:

"I want to talk to you, my father and my mother,"
    he said,
"For I cannot call you by any other name, given that
You received me and accepted me as your son.
I want you to know that I have not changed a bit;
My heart and Warigia's beat to the same rhythm.

"But deep inside I feel I cannot abide by your law,
    that
Husband and wife must live in this region to be
    near you,
Because, though the heart is willing to stay here,
It also feels the pull of home, where I came from,
    and I ask that
You allow me to take Warigia home for her to
    know my parents."

"You have done well to let me know your heart,"
    Gĩkũyũ said,

"For it is true, the word locked up inside cannot
    win an argument.
Your words have stung my heart as a parent;
Children who remember their parents are blessed;
As future parents, they will expect the same from
    their offspring.

"But in my house there is no law for the lamb and
    another for a sheep.
That was why I told you about the law before your
    hearts had found each other.
Those who were unable to abide by it went away, in
    peace.
I cannot prevent you from doing what your heart
    tells you,
But Warigia will not be separated from her siblings."

Kīhara looked at Warigia as if his heart had been
    hit with a club.
Then he took a few steps, determined to go, but then
He stopped and looked back as if he would change
    his mind.
He did this a few times—stop, look, and go—but
    finally walked toward the gate.
Warigia could not believe that Kīhara would leave
    her, and she spoke out:

"My heart is full of love for you all, my sisters,"
    Warigia said, and
For my father and mother especially, for they gave
    birth to me, gave me my life,
And I had sworn never to leave them here alone, but
I too do not agree with this law, because
These suitors are human like me, and they left their
    place, for us.

"You too, my father and mother, came from someplace.
God brought you here, and you built a home here at
    Mūkūrūweinī.
If I stay, I will grow old thinking that mother is the
    only one who cooks well.
I, too, will follow the dictates of my heart, the same
    way you once did.
I will go out in the world to find my own Mūkūrū-
    weinī."

Warigia did not wait for her father or mother to
    respond.
She feared her heart would soften, for she truly loved
    them.
From birth, she knew no other lives but those of her
    parents and siblings,

But loyalty to the heart triumphed. She followed it
　　without once looking back.
Her sisters followed her, singing sorrowfully the sad
　　song of farewell:

*Stay, stay,*
*Stay!*
*Stay and please*
*Don't do this to me.*
*Stay!*
*It's more than I can bear.*
*Stay,*
*Our Warigia dear,*
*Stay!*
*You promised never to leave me.*
*Stay—*
*And now you're going away.*

The song they had sung escorting the other brides
Was now pregnant with the deep sorrow of parting
　　forever.
They followed her, but after Warigia disappeared in
　　the distance, they came back.
Gĩkũyũ and Mũmbi looked as if they had lost their
　　voices,

But they also saw themselves in the actions of
   Warigia, for

She had done as they had once done,
Followed the dictates of her heart,
Her action reminding them of the past drumbeat
   of their own hearts.
Although in their case it was disaster, that made
   them undertake their journey,
Still they felt Warigia had taken after them.


*Gĩkũyũ said:*
"Peace, God the Giver Supreme, look after those
   two.
When the sun becomes too hot, lead them to cool
   shade.
When it rains and storms, lead them to a shelter.
If they encounter a dangerous animal,
Close its eyes so it does not see them.
Remove out of their way holes, illnesses, and ogres.
Wherever they end up, they are my children."


*Mũmbi said:*
"May it be so. Peace!
Peace, that they may always take the middle way.
Peace, that they too will bear me grandchildren."

## 22

# Warigia
# and the
# Lion

The families of the Nine increased.
They tamed more virgin land.
They raised cattle and goats that yielded much
    milk.
They brought even more land under cultivation.
The crops yielded good harvests; their granaries
    were full.

But nothing brought them as much joy as when
All the nine felt life stir inside them.
All the nine wombs started expanding,
And they knew for sure they now carried the yolk
    of life.

It was amazing, this miracle of a life carrying an-
    other life,
Which moved inside their own bodies, reminding
    them what Gĩkũyũ said,
That woman is the mother of all human life, male
    or female,

That all children should always remember to love
    and respect their parents,
And especially their mother, who carried them for
    nine months with love.

When the children began to come out of mothers'
    bellies,
A new joy would burst in the homestead:
Five ululations for a boy;
Five ululations for a girl.
Boy and girl make our tomorrow.

They prepared a big feast to celebrate the new nine.
They also created new songs, new lullabies.
Drums, flutes, and jingles were ready,
All to celebrate the mix of girls and boys,
The House of Mūmbi begun in a man and a woman.

Just as they were about to begin feasting,
A lion appeared at the entrance to the yard.
The beast stood on its hind legs
As if about to jump and attack them.
The men rushed for their spears,

But Gīkūyū ordered them to pause, because
No lion had ever visited the house,

Whether through the front or back entrance.
Then the beast removed its mane,
And at first they were at a loss for words,
Before suddenly bursting into screams of joy.


It was Warigia at the gate,
Her tummy big and round.
But just before they could ask her about the lion-
    wear,
Birth pangs began, the life inside asking to be let
    out.
The feast to celebrate the new nine became a cele-
    bration a new Perfect Nine.

*Later, Warigia said:*
"I am happy with the way you have received me.
You didn't take away the bridge to cross back to
    you,
Confirming the truth of the saying, 'Don't burn
    your bridges.'
Ever since I was a child,
I have aspired to walk in the footsteps of Gīkūyū
    and Mūmbi,

"Follow the paths you have followed,
Drink from the calabash you have drunk from,

Wash in the waters you have washed in,
But desires of the heart do not always dictate the
    outcome,
Or mature in the way one had dreamed.

"About my legs, you all know:
A body of an adult on the legs of a baby.
When you, my siblings, went to hunt,
I remained at home, weeping.
Then I resolved to be the best of me.
I started to teach myself to shoot with arrows.

"I trained by targeting posts or even birds,
Until my eyes learned to see a path in the air,
So much so that when I aimed and let an arrow
    go,
It followed the path my eyes had already mapped
    out.
And when you returned from your hunts, I would
    hide my arrows.

"I even tried climbing up trees, also jumping,
Just to test how high or far I could reach with those
    legs.
You all know how much I strove to do things for
    myself.

Disability of the body does not mean disability of
the heart and mind.
The heart and the head rule the body.

"When my eyes first fell on the one you named
Kĩhara,
I felt my heart beat so hard, I said, 'This is the one.'
Even after he had joined you in the journey to the
mountain,
I always felt that he and I were for each other.
At the river, I would hear his voice in the water.

"That was why I would crawl there every day and sit
on a rock;
And I would hear him murmuring to me, take cour-
age.
Sometimes his voice would tell me to play in the water;
And I did as he urged me, playing in the water,
Trying to run with the water or against the flow of
the river.

"When I first felt a bit of power in my legs, I didn't
dare to believe it.
Then I saw I was able to stand up in the water.
I started wading in the river, my arms raised toward
my man.

Then I tried walking on the dry earth, and I felt the
  legs hold.
That day I came home to my parents walking on
  firm legs.

"After that, you finally came back from the moun-
  tain,
And I learned that the day I walked home on my
  legs
Was also the day my man plucked the hair that
  cures from the jaws of an ogre.
And that miracle confirmed my heart's choice; he
  was the one for me.
That was why, when he said he would leave, I fol-
  lowed him.

"I found him standing a little distance from the
  gate,
Undecided between going away and coming back
And again beg my father to change his mind.
When his eyes fell on mine, he came back to life.
A bird with one wing had regained the second
  wing.

"What more can I tell you?
It's true we flew with our newfound wings,

That we encountered many tribulations,
Ogres and wild animals chasing us,
But nothing would weaken my man's resolve.
He would share whatever he had learned from your
    journey to the mountain.

"We went through and across many regions in many
    days.
Finally, at the edge of a forest, he pointed at smoke
    from his people's home.
Suddenly a lion emerged from nowhere and jumped
    toward me.
As quickly as my man jumped on it before it could
    reach me.
They struggled, man and lion, in a brutal wrestling
    of the human and the brute.

"I really don't know from where my man got the
    power, but
In the end he was able to plunge a spear into it.
I heard the lion roar. It left my man alone and ran away.
Oh, my sisters, when I reached him, he looked at me,
    and

"He managed to say just one thing: 'Go back home.'
And then he fell into final silence.

I struggled and managed to bury the body;
And then I sat there alone, and tears would not
  come.
Even thinking of what to do next was difficult.

"Still undecided, I cast my eyes in the direction the
  lion had taken.
I saw it in the bush, and it was looking at me.
I remembered what you always told me, that when a
  lion tastes blood,
It behaves as if its thirst for blood has increased, and
I started trying to figure out how I could escape its
  deadly desires.

"Before I took a few steps away from it, I felt a tick-
  ling sensation and I looked back:
The beast, the spear still protruding from its body,
Was running toward me to end my life the way it
  did my man's.
Quick on my feet, I reached for my bow and arrows
  and rained arrows on it.
The barrage made the beast halt, and then it ran
  into the forest.

"This lion, which has just killed my man, will not
  stop killing humans.

I will hunt it up and down forests and valleys, I
    resolved.
I, Warigia, will follow it to the end of the world if
    necessary.
I collected my man's arrows.
I hung both quivers on my back and plunged into
    the forest.

"I followed the trail of blood;
Day and night I followed it.
And then one morning I saw the beast lying in the
    grass.
I was tired but I felt power resurge in me.

"I looked for a tree with twin stems branching
    out.
I hid behind it, and through the gap between the
    stems, I shot at it.
The lion jumped up, and, now furious, it came
    toward me.
It got caught in the gap, and I used my spear to
    good effect.

"After it fell, I removed its skin
And carried it on my shoulders and looked for a
    way back.

Then I got an idea: I would cover myself with the
    lion's skin.
Yes, the skin of the beast that took my man from
    me
Would make other animals and ogres leave me
    alone.

"I also derived hope from thinking that the spirit
    of my man was with me.
I was, after all, the proud daughter of Gĩkũyũ and
    Mũmbi,
The Warigia or Wanjũgũ who made the nine into
    the Perfect Nine.
So here I am with the head and the skin of the lion
    that killed my man,

"So that when the new life you welcomed
With ululations of joy grows up,
I will show him the trophy, proof that
His father died for love—of
His parents, his wife, and his people."

23

# Cementing
# Relations
# Between
# In-Laws

Gĩkũyũ and Mũmbi and all those gathered there
Were shocked by the tragedy that took Warigia's
   man
But also amazed by the courage of him and
   Warigia.
They decided that, in order to commemorate the
   man and also
The return of Warigia alive, matrimonial rites
   would include a few additions.

## The Ceremony for the Union of the Two Families

The family of the groom carries gifts to the family
of the bride.
During the feast, the groom hangs a necklace round
the neck of the woman
Amid songs, dances, drums, and flutes.
After some time, the family of the bride carries gifts
to the family of the groom.
During the feast, the bride ties a beaded leather
band on the arm of the man
Amid songs, dances, drums, and flutes, an orchestra
of voices and instruments.
The two ceremonies are for uniting the two families
and communities.
The two feasts add to the rites of wooing and be-
trothal.

*The Ceremony for Enabling the New Home*

Ceremonies for enabling a good start for the couple
    follow on another day.
Both families contribute to the new couple,
Just as Gĩkũyũ and Mũmbi did to the nine and
    their men,
Gifting them with the seeds for starting a new
    home.

24

Epilogue:
The
Will of
Gĩkũyũ
and
Mũmbi

Nine months after the return of Warigia to her
    parents,
Gĩkũyũ and Mũmbi called for a gathering of the
    Perfect Nine,
Together with their husbands and their children.
They ate food and drank porridge, and they sang
    and beat drums in joy.
In the evening, just before dark, Gĩkũyũ spoke to
    the gathering:

*Gĩkũyũ said:*
"Now all of you can see that gray hair has covered
    our heads;
Even our voices have lost strength.
The arm has not the power to throw a spear or hold
    a sword.
Our eyes can no longer see the target in the game of
    arrows, but we are blessed:
You, the Perfect Nine, have given us the foundation
    of nine clans, the Perfect Nine.

. . .

"But our time has come.
Tomorrow we are going on a journey.
We are going back to the mountain from which we
    came.
In case we don't return, I leave you with these
    words:

"Don't look for me in wicked deeds.
Don't look for me in theft and robbery.
Don't look for me in idleness.
Don't look for me in senseless violence.
Don't look for me in hatred.
Don't look for me in meaningless wars.
Don't look for me in bloodletting strife,
For my name must not be in the mouths
Of those plotting wicked deeds."

*Mũmbi said:*
"Look for me in the water.
Look for me in the wind.
Look for me in the soil.
Look for me in the fire—
Even in the sun,
Even in the stars.
Look for me in the rain.

Look for me among the tillers.
Look for me in the harvests.

"Look for me in love.
Look for me in unity.
Look for me among the helping.
Look for me among the oppressed.
Look for me among the seekers of justice,
Those who give food to the hungry, water to the
    thirsty.
Look for me among those helping the ailing.
Look for me among them without clothes and
    shelter.
Look for me among those building the nation in
    the name of the human."

*Gĩkũyũ and Mũmbi said in unison:*
"If you do that,
We are together with you
Now and all the days, life without end."

# Acknowledgments

THIS STORY HAS BEEN TOLD AND RETOLD as part of the lore of the Gĩkũyũ people. I have gained a lot from all of those tellings. I would like to thank the following for their input into my retelling and interpretation: Njeeri wa Ngũgĩ; Njaũ wa Njoroge and Wambũi; Mũkoma wa Ngũgĩ; Wanjikũ wa Kabĩra; Kĩmani wa Njogu; Kĩarie Kamau; Kĩmani wa Nyoro; and Julius Maina. And thank you Emmanuel Kariũki for your research that traces the origins of Bantu peoples to Ancient Egypt. And you, Kamoji Wachira, thank you for our many talks on languages and the development of Kenya and Africa and on the migrations of African peoples.

penguin.co.uk/vintage